MW00638065

Gardens of Italy

Gardens of Italy

Ann Larås

special photography by

Åke E:son Lindman

FRANCES LINCOLN

CONTENTS

LAZIO 18

CAMPANIA 72

TUSCANY 100

Frances Lincoln Limited
4 Torriano Mews, Torriano Avenue
London NW5 2RZ
www.franceslincoln.com

Gardens of Italy

First Frances Lincoln edition 2005

A catalogue record for this book is available from the British Library.

Printed and bound in Singapore

ISBN 0 7112 2490 0

9 8 7 6 5 4 3 2 1

Page 1 One of the many beautiful sculptures of dogs at Villa Gamberaia, Settignano.
Page 2 The water parterre at Villa Gamberaia.

VENETO 140

LIGURIA 156

LOMBARDY & PIEDMONT 164

MAPS OF ITALY

Abruzzo
CITTÀ D. VATICANO
ROMA
Tèrmoli
L. di Lèsina
L. di Varano
Rodi Gargànico
Vieste
MAR ADRIÀTICO
Molise
Làzio
Frosinone
Isèrnia
CAMPOBASSO
Manfredònia
Latina
Fòggia
Trani
BARI
Benevento
Caserta
Campània
Melfi
Pùglia
Ìsole Ponziane
NÀPOLI
Avellino
Pozzuoli
Castellammare di Stàbia
POTENZA
Matera
Brìndisi
Ì d'Ìschia
Sorrento
Salerno
Basilicata
Tàranto
Lecce
Ì di Capri
Metaponto
Òtranto
Agri
Gallìpoli
Palinuro
Sìbari
MAR TIRRENO
Calàbria
Cosenza
Crotone
Lamèzia Terme
CATANZARO
Ìsole Eòlie
Vibo Valèntia
Ì. di Ùstica
Milazzo
Messina
Locri
PALERMO
Règgio di Calàbria
MAR IÒNIO
Tràpani
Cefalù
Alcamo
Tèrmini Imerese
Taormina
Ìsole Ègadi
Marsala
Sicìlia
Acireale
Caltanissetta
Enna
Catània
Sciacca
Caltagirone
Agrigento
Salso
Ìsole Pelàgie
Siracusa
Gela
Ì. di Lampedusa
Ragusa
Ì di Pantelleria
Noto
MAR MEDITERRÀNEO

FOREWORD by Ann Larås

Opposite Every June, around the feast of Corpus Christi, the sloping main street of the town of Genzano di Roma is decorated with a floral carpet created using fifty tons of flowers, arranged in intricate patterns.

My aim in this book is to share my joy in Italy's gardens. The gardens described in the pages that follow have been grouped into six sections, which cover different Italian regions from the lake districts of the north to the Amalfi coast in the south: Lazio, Campania, Tuscany, Veneto, Liguria, and Lombardy and Piedmont. They represent a cross-section of the green treasures created in Italy during a period of five hundred years, from the Renaissance designs of the sixteenth century through to the modern schemes of the twentieth.

Near Rome, for example, there are grand Renaissance water gardens such as Pirro Ligorio's spectacular Villa d'Este, but there is also Russell Page's flowering landscape garden, laid out in the twentieth century. In the section on Tuscany I have, of course, included the Medici family's villas, alongside examples of the varied gardens designed around Florence during the twentieth century by the prolific and versatile Pietro Porcinai. In the section on the Veneto, I focus on Giardino Giusti in Verona, but also feature a Palladian estate, the Villa Barbaro at Maser, and the Modernist garden of the Palazzo Querini Stampalia in Venice, which was created by Carlo Scarpa in the 1950s.

The book has no ambitions to be seen as a comprehensive study. I look at thirty gardens and parks in detail and describe an additional thirty more briefly, but because of limitations of space I have had, reluctantly, to leave out many other glorious examples. I hope that in the future I will have a chance to explore those, too. In selecting whether a garden should be included I took into account not only its beauty but also whether it is well kept, its accessibility to the public, and the extent to which it is representative of its era. Of course, I was also influenced by my own tastes and interests.

My research took me on a journey through garden architecture and botany, with excursions into history, art and philosophy. Many of the country estates and their gardens are located in places that are difficult to reach but also some of the most scenic in all of Italy – on hillsides and in ravines, often situated high up with magnificent views across farmland, forests or water. And travelling on the back roads through the Italian countryside – past vineyards, cornfields or slopes covered with poppies – is itself an experience not to be forgotten.

Italians have a close relationship with plants. Flowers play an important role on formal occasions – at parties and religious ceremonies, at weddings, funerals and confirmations – but they are also part of everyday life. Every village or town has balconies with a profusion of flowers or terraces with lemon trees in pots. A door facing the street is often framed by shocking pink bougainvillea or scented jasmine; ivy covers the walls or is trained to climb up pine trees. As you walk through a bustling city, you may even come across a fig tree that has seeded in a crack between pavement and wall.

One of many beautiful memories I have related to flowers is of a chance visit to the best-preserved ancient building in Rome – the Pantheon. When I arrived a Mass was in progress, with wonderful music, and at the end of the ceremony tens of thousands of rose petals showered down through the 9-metre (30-foot) opening in the dome. It was an enchanting surprise. Another flower memory is from the town of Genzano di Roma in the Alban hills, where people from all over the world gather for the annual flower festival. The long main street between the square and the church was decorated, in the Italian tradition, with a carpet of flower petals forming intricate patterns.

During my research I interviewed experts and gardeners and met many enthusiastic owners. Many of the villas have been owned by the same family for hundreds of years, so the owners are often the descendants of the cardinal or pope, businessman or politician, immigrant Briton or American who originally created the garden. I was eager to find answers to many questions. How is it possible to preserve a garden for as long as half a millennium? What is the motivation behind this hard and sometimes thankless work? Where do the knowledge, energy and money necessary to look after a historic garden come from? The answers were always interesting and thought-provoking, sometimes surprising.

I hope that you will find this book inspiring, and that reading it will give you as much pleasure as researching and writing it has given me.

The Canopus, the long canal at Hadrian's Villa. The Roman Emperor Hadrian created his country estate in Tivoli, east of Rome, in AD 123–134.

The Gardens of Antiquity

To understand Italian Renaissance gardens, it is necessary first to look briefly at the gardens of the ancient Roman Empire, which provided their basis and inspiration. Roman gardens took elements from the earlier traditions of the Near East, Hellenistic gardens and Persian hunting parks, the paradise gardens or *paradeisoi* – from the Old Persian *pairi* (enclosed) and *daeza* (wall) – and shaped them into a synthesis that was uniquely Roman.

There were two principal types of Roman garden. One was the country garden set in the landscape, for example the gardens at Emperor Hadrian's Villa in Tivoli near Rome. The other was the peristyle garden, an open inner courtyard garden surrounded by a covered walk flanked with supporting columns which was an integral part of a town dwelling – almost like another room. Here I will look in a little more detail at some superb examples of Roman gardens: the Villa of Livia, in Prima Porta, north of Rome, and the gardens of Pompeii. Both sites can be visited and studied today.

The Villa of Livia

The Villa of Livia, traditionally the home of Livia Drusilla (58 BC–AD 29), wife of the Emperor Augustus, is situated on a hill seven miles north of Rome, in what today is the suburb of Prima Porta. This Imperial country estate was created on a plateau with views across the countryside and with Rome visible in the distance. Excavations began in

1863. Italian archaeologists discovered the peristyle in 1982 and it was excavated in 1997–8 by Swedish archaeologists in collaboration with the Sopraintendenza Archeologica di Roma.

The Villa of Livia was also known as the *villa ad gallinas albas*. The story is told by Pliny the Elder (AD 23–79) in his natural history, *Naturalis Historia*. According to the legend, an eagle flying over the garden dropped its prey – a white chicken, *gallina alba*, with a laurel branch in its beak. The laurel branch fell into the lap of the newly married Livia and it was seen as an omen. The chicken became a chicken farm and the laurel branch grew into a laurel grove. From these trees triumphal wreaths were made to crown the heads of victorious generals returning to Rome in glory.

It is easy to imagine the Empress Livia looking out across her little peristyle garden from one of the small rooms that surrounded it. The peristyle covered an area of only about 55 square metres (590 square feet). Marble Ionic columns, probably arranged in a pattern of 5 x 7, framed a central courtyard. Evergreens such as box, myrtle, bay laurel and ivy played an important role in the Roman garden, and it is probable that Livia's small garden had a formal layout with a path and clipped box hedges, interspersed with statues and maybe some oleander bushes. A plinth discovered in the middle of the garden is thought to be the base of a fountain. The little garden was probably planted with small trees and there may have been climbers growing up the columns. There may also have been citrus trees in pots and maybe an odd rose or a violet.

Archaeologists have found in Livia's garden fragments of some sixty planting pots, of two main types. One type, with a single hole at the bottom, is thought to have been used for plants grown from seedlings at early garden nurseries. The other kind of pot had, in addition to the bottom hole, another three holes in its side. It is thought that these pots were used for propagation. A branch from a tree would be layered in a soil-filled pot. When it had rooted, the branch was cut off and the new tree, still in its pot, was planted in the ground.

Among the most important archaeological finds at the Villa of Livia were the wonderful frescoes depicting abundantly flowering landscape with exotic birds (and an exquisite birdcage) which decorated the underground dining room or *triclinium*.

A fresco from the Villa of Livia, painted in the first century BC. This fresco was one of four wall paintings that decorated the walls of the remarkable underground dining room at the Villa of Livia in Prima Porta. They depict paradisiacal botanical elements including small trees, plants and exotic birds. According to a botanical analysis made in 2003, the following twenty-four plant species are represented: the strawberry tree (*Arbutus unedo*), bay laurel (*Laurus nobilis*), oleander (*Nerium oleander*), holm oak (*Quercus ilex*), English oak (*Q. robur*), Cornelian cherry (*Cornus mas*), myrtle (*Myrtus communis*), hart's-tongue fern (*Asplenium scolopendrium*), early dog violet (*Viola riviniana*), crown daisy (*Chrysanthemum coronarium*), stinking chamomile (*Anthemis cotula*), Italian cypress (*Cupressus sempervirens*), quince (*Cydonia oblonga*), stone pine (*Pinus pinea*), pomegranate (*Punica granatum*), opium poppy (*Papaver somniferum*), cabbage rose (*Rosa centifolia*) and date palm (*Phoenix dactylifera*).

They were discovered in the villa in 1863 and were moved in 1955 to the Museo Nazionale, which is now housed at Palazzo Massimo alle Terme in Rome.

Slightly further away from the house is a larger garden usually referred to as the garden terrace. The north-eastern corner of the garden terrace was excavated in 1997–9. An area of more than 280 square metres (3000 square feet) was examined in minute detail. Here were found small pieces of ceramics, brick and stucco, traces of roots, amphorae, thin-walled pottery, lamps and some metal objects. Shells, presumably used to improve drainage, were also found in the soil. In the same corner of the garden terrace the archaeologists found remains of walls and evidence for the existence of a portico. The geophysical surveys showed three parallel walls with channels between them. There are compartments which were presumably used for planting beds and traces which indicate the likely existence of three apses. It also seems probable that there was a hanging garden, probably irrigated by an aqueduct which came from the hilltop north of the villa. The aqueduct came to light when the tunnel for the modern Via Flaminia was excavated through the hill.

Preserved in ashes

It happened in the year AD 79, at the beginning of the reign of the new Emperor Titus – the terrible volcanic eruption that destroyed the city of Pompeii, north of Naples. The city was totally buried in ash, stones and lava. Ironically, the disaster that destroyed Pompeii also preserved the city. It is thanks to the volcano that we have a clear picture today of what Pompeii would have looked like in the first century AD. When the archaeologists began to excavate Pompeii in the mid-eighteenth century, it became clear that the ash and lava had preserved house foundations, objects and paintings. The amphitheatre and temples were excavated, along with private houses, workshops, shops, bakeries and taverns. There were fascinating discoveries including sophisticated water hydraulics and, most famous and perhaps most interesting of all, the wonderful frescoes with their rich motifs – often exotic birds and flowers – in strong pigments, Pompeian red and heavenly blue.

On a day in the middle of March 2004, the excavation site of Pompeii is neither too hot nor too cold. A few tourists are moving about led by tour guides. The earth is

Above left A wall painting of a garland in the richly decorated Villa of Mysteries, situated outside the city walls.
Above right The atrium of a Pompeian house, with the square central basin to collect rainwater. The peristyle garden opens off the reception room behind.

coming alive and there are narcissi flowering under the apple trees on a gentle slope. The Roman walls are in danger of being pulled apart by ivy climbing up the ruins. Although the ivy-clad walls look beautiful, it is sad to see the ancient stone being destroyed by the strong roots. There are blue rosemary flowers on the slopes, and down by the amphitheatre vineyards have been planted with vines of the type that would have been grown by the ancient Romans. The rows of supports look rather elegant in the low morning sunlight.

The driving force behind the new plantings and the excavations of Pompeii is a leading authority on garden archaeology, the American Professor Wilhelmina Jashemski of the University of Maryland. Professor Jashemski has conducted excavations and studied the gardens of Pompeii since the 1970s, and she has found traces of 450 private gardens and public plantings. Pompeii was a green town.

The peristyle gardens that are to be seen in many of the private dwellings in the centre of Pompeii give some insight into how a Roman garden of the first century AD would have looked. The houses were often planned so that there was a clear view straight through the building. In the first area after the entrance there would be a courtyard (*atrium*), with a square basin (*impluvium*) in the middle to collect rainwater from a hole in the ceiling (*compluvium*). The water then fell into the cistern (*puteus*), to be used throughout the house. There may have been a few plants in pots on the paving stones. The small rooms around the atrium (*cubiculae*) were often used as sleeping chambers. The walls of the atrium would usually have been covered with frescoes, which were often intended to extend the garden by creating the illusion of a view. This *trompe l'oeil* technique continued to be used during the Renaissance. Sometimes the paintings did not stop at representing fountains, fishponds, trees, birds and flowers, but included complete landscapes with mountains, lakes and wild animals.

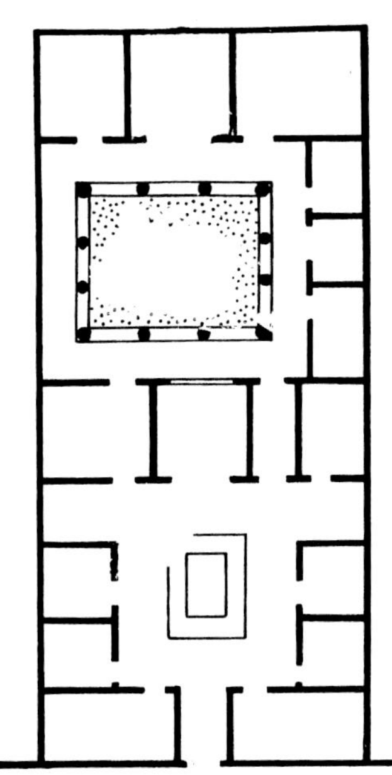

Above left Drawing by E.M. Pinto Guillaume showing a reconstruction of the peristyle at the Villa of Livia.
Above right A plan showing the basic layout of a peristyle house in Pompeii.

Via the reception room – *tablinum* – I reach the peristyle, which is the most social area of the house. The dining room – *triclinium* – and the guest rooms – *oeci* – would have surrounded the peristyle. The atrium and the peristyle were used for receiving guests; other parts of the house were more private.

Archaeologists have used various methods to investigate which types of plants and trees grew in the Pompeian garden, making casts from root cavities (preserved because they were filled with pumice during the eruption), as well as analysing traces of pollen in the soil and carbonized fruits and seeds. These examinations have shown that the following trees grew in Pompeii: chestnuts, olives, figs, laurels, oleanders and fruit trees including pomegranates, quinces, pears, apples, almonds and cherries. Pliny the Elder writes that lemon trees were imported in pots with holes for the roots. There is evidence of at least one fig tree which was planted near a latrine, probably so that the low branches would hide people from view. Columns and pillars were sometimes covered in garlands of ivy. Evergreen plants were clipped into different shapes by gardeners known as *topiarii*. In the first century AD Pompeii had a good supply of water via an aqueduct leading in to the town.

Pliny the Elder himself perished at Pompeii, but one of those who survived the eruption was his nephew, Pliny the Younger (AD 63–113). The younger Pliny's *Letters* are among the most important sources of information about the villas and gardens of Antiquity, and they were a great source of inspiration to the learned and sophisticated men who created the gardens of Renaissance Italy. It all started with Pliny's description of the concept of the villa, which my friend landscape architect Thorbjörn Andersson examines in detail in the following pages.

Ann Larås

INTRODUCTION by Thorbjörn Andersson

Today, the word villa is often used to refer to a suburban family house. In the Italy of the Renaissance it meant something very different. Following a pattern established in Ancient Rome, the Italian Renaissance villa was essentially the place outside the city limits where the rich and powerful could recuperate in private from the pressures of everyday life. In the city, they would have their town house – their *palazzo*. The villa was its complement. It was rooted in the countryside, a harmonious unit of building, garden and landscape, a work of art in which all the different parts were in perfect balance. The garden was as important as the house and represented its extension into the landscape. Much attention was paid to the edicts of Pliny the Younger, who in his *Letters* sets out instructions for what one should think of when building a villa, how the surrounding area should be considered, the slopes, the winds, the shade, the plants and the views.

Pliny also describes how he enjoys *otium cum dignitate* at his country estate. *Otium*, leisure, represents the calm, undisturbed life – the opposite of *negotium*, which is the worldly business by which one earns one's living, in the city. No business is to be done at the villa. It is a safe haven for a gentleman, maybe even his paradise on earth. Among the nobility of Renaissance Italy, this developed into a social pattern known as *villeggiatura*, or withdrawing to the country.

Renaissance means rebirth: the rebirth of the ideals of Greek and Roman Antiquity. Philosophy and science were studied with renewed enthusiasm and the Platonic academy was reborn. In the gardens of Villa Careggi, north of Florence, the members of a Neoplatonic academy studied, among other things, nature and plants: one of its members, Bernardo Telesio, is reported to have said: 'I can learn more from studying a piece of grass than from studying everything in all the books in the world.'

The core business of Renaissance Florence was banking. The bankers could amass a concentration of capital, and much of it was used for vast building projects on the slopes of the River Arno outside Florence. The most famous of these bankers were the members of the Medici family, who commissioned many of the most splendid of the villas we visit today. The Medici were also, of course, patrons of the arts and sponsors of promising artists, architects and poets. They and other patrons supported their protégés by commissioning them not only to work on their villas, but also both to enhance and to describe the life that went on there.

The Villa Medici in Fiesole is built on a steep slope with views across Florence. This classical Renaissance villa was designed *c.*1458–61 by Michelozzo Michelozzi for Cosimo de'Medici I, following the precepts laid down by Pliny the Younger in his *Letters*. The current layout of the garden is more recent: one of the terraces was designed in 1911 by architect Cecil Pinsent for Lady Sybil Cutting. She lived in the Villa Medici with her daughter, Iris – who later, as Iris Origo, created the garden at La Foce (see page 108).

The Renaissance was a high point for science. The hegemony of the Church was about to be broken – spiritual power was facing competition from secular power. Meanwhile, Church officials also created their own paradise on earth. One of the most famous villas, Villa d'Este (see page 34), was built by Cardinal Ippolito II d'Este, and the driving force is said to have been revenge. The Cardinal had made a tactical mistake in his career: he had been away in France when he might have been wiser to stay close to the Vatican, and when the old Pope died and the new one was chosen he was overlooked. But with his new villa in Tivoli outside Rome, he was going to show them all. For the cooling water jokes at Villa d'Este, the water from the river was directed to become an underground stream supplying fountains, cascades, basins, jets, ponds and canals. It is still today the most exquisite water garden in the world.

The Italian villa tradition has been passed on throughout the centuries. It reached its peak during the Renaissance, but the idea of a garden, a building and a landscape forming an inseparable unit survives in examples from later eras. Another special feature of the Italian villas is that they have often been owned by the same family for hundreds of years. This means that the villas have been preserved and looked after; traditions have been handed on. We can still travel to Tuscany, to the Lazio, to Campania or to Lake Como in the mountains north of Milan, and see historic villas perched high on the sloping hillsides. There it is still possible to enjoy *otium cum dignitate* – leisure with dignity.

LAZIO

A RENAISSANCE GEM
DESIGNED BY GIACOMO BAROZZI DA VIGNOLA FOR GIANFRANCESCO GAMBARA
FROM 1566

Villa Lante

Bagnaia

It is early evening. The siesta is over and the Cardinal's guests enjoy a stroll in the garden. It is still hot but the fountains are sending out refreshing bursts of cool air. Meanwhile, the host is preparing an *al fresco* dinner party on the Giant's Terrace. Wine is being cooled in the water channel of the stone table, while the kitchen staff are balancing plates piled high with delicacies; pheasant filled with pomegranates, artichokes and olives of every kind.

This is how I imagine *la dolce vita* on a hot summer's day in the mid-sixteenth century. The young Cardinal Gianfrancesco Gambara has guests to stay at his country estate in Bagnaia to the east of Viterbo. Gambara was a man of culture and a lover of nature, and he had created a fashionable garden. This garden was intended to realize the dream of the gardens of Antiquity, and be a place for feasts, ceremonies and plays.

What has attracted visitors to this part of Lazio throughout time is the fresh water. The name Bagnaia has the same origin as the word *bagno* (bath), and already in Roman times the area was well known for its mineral water. The village of Bagnaia lies on a ridge of volcanic stone, with a view of the Cimini mountains. The small thirteenth-century village with its narrow lanes and roughly built stone houses has kept its medieval feeling. As in most Italian villages, there is a square in the centre with small shops, a fountain, a café and a few benches where villagers gather to watch the street and the passers-by. The Via Jacopo Barozzi leads up to the entrance of Villa Lante and the Fountain of Pegasus, protector of the forest, and the water nymphs. This is the wild part of Villa Lante, used as a hunting ground for centuries. During the fifteenth century one of the keenest hunters, Cardinal Riario, built himself a hunting lodge. It still stands, surrounded by dense forest, meandering pathways and a fountain or two covered in green moss.

Pages 18–19 View over the village of Tivoli from the magnificent water garden of Villa d'Este.

Opposite The Fountain of the Flood, set between two pavilions on the top terrace, is the source of water for the whole garden at Villa Lante.

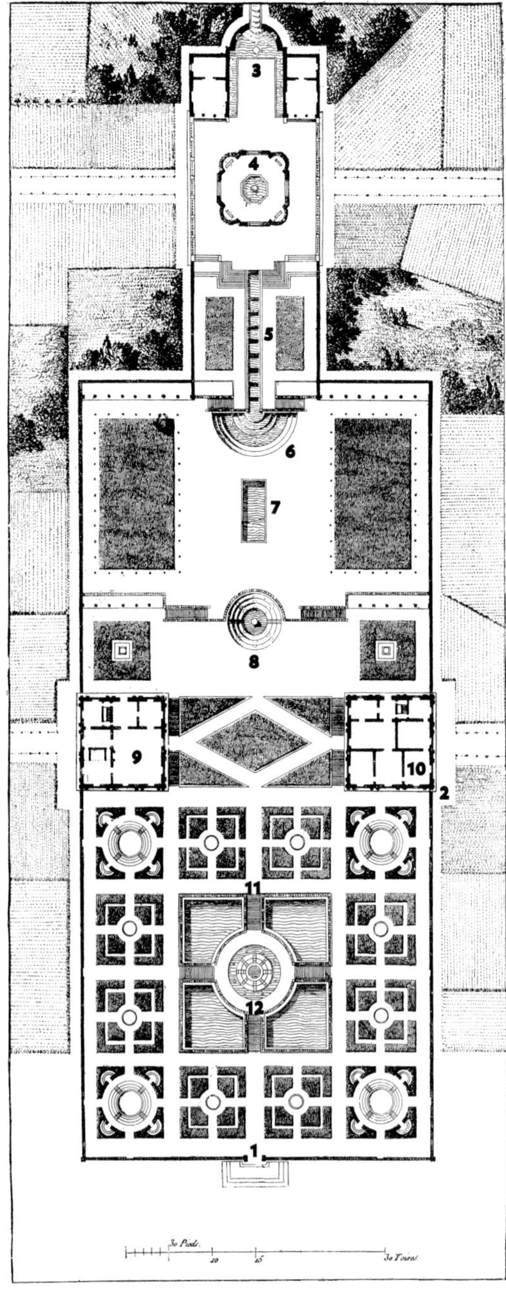

1 Historic entrance
2 Modern entrance
3 Fountain of the Flood
4 Fountain of the Dolphins
5 Fountain of the Chain
6 Fountain of the Giants
7 Fountain of the Lamps
8 Fountain of the Table
9 Montalto casino
10 Lante casino
11 Lake garden
12 Fountain of the Moors

Giovanni Francesco Gambara was consecrated as Bishop of Viterbo in 1566 by Pope Pius V. In the same year, Gambara hired the famous architect Giacomo Barozzi da Vignola, who had created a magnificent garden at the Villa Farnese in nearby Caprarola (see page 54). An artist and an architect, Vignola was fascinated by the laws of perspective and by Roman and Greek art. His commission was to design a summer palace with gardens and parks, 'the beauty of which had never been seen in its time'. Its main rival was Villa d'Este high in the mountains outside Rome (see page 34).

The garden should be explored as was intended: from the top downwards, like a symbolic journey from the source of life to the sea of death. Once past the entrance, take the steps up to the top terrace, without turning around. According to Giovannino Fatica, the curator and architect responsible for the Villa Lante (now State-run), the garden has three or five terraces, 'depending on how you count'.

'I prefer the top part of the garden, where formality meets the forest. This is where I can feel the magic of the place. In the sixteenth century magic was a branch of learning,' says Fatica. 'It was a serious form of art, with the aim of drawing energy from nature.'

A journey from the top downwards. At the back of the top terrace, between two pavilions, is the main water source for the whole garden, the Fountain of the Flood, created by Vignola as a symbol of the spring of life. From the fountain, water originating in the clear springs of Monte Sant'Angelo flows down into the garden in a straight line, cutting through the terraces, until it finally comes to rest in the lake parterre.

Two proud mottled plane trees, each 3 metres (10 feet) in circumference, guard the flanks of the top terrace. Their roots have torn the ground open. In an alcove of box

hedges in the middle of the terrace is the octagonal Fountain of the Dolphins, glimmering like copper although it is in fact *peperino*, a local volcanic stone. The water disappears underground and re-emerges at the mouth of a crayfish (*gambero*), an allusion to the coat of arms of the Gambara family. The water chain, like a mountain stream, takes the water further at high speed; the bottom is cleverly designed so as to be uneven, to make the water dance. It cascades down the flight of steps and tumbles into the Fountain of the Giants, where it comes to rest for a while by the lazily reclining river gods. A hidden pipe of terracotta carries the water to a channel running through the middle of a stone table, where drinks were placed to keep them cool. This was the dining room for special occasions.

The water jets are demonstrated by Giovannino Fatica, who opens a heavy stone trap door in the ground, revealing pipes and taps. All mechanics and effects are worked from there. The Cardinal, who clearly had a sense of humour, used to entertain the guests and himself with the *giochi d'acqua* – 'water jokes'. When a servant turned the taps, the guests were splashed with water from hidden water spouts. The water could come from ahead, from below or from the side, and you can imagine the surprise of the guests, presumably dressed in their finest clothes, at the sudden showers. Some water jets are still in working order today and if you are lucky (or unlucky!) the staff may well show them to you.

Cardinal Gambara was criticized for his frivolity and extravagance. In 1580 the saintly Cardinal Carlo Borromeo came to view the villa and the garden. He remained silent throughout the walkabout, and when Gambara finally asked him for his opinion, he said: 'Cardinal Gambara, you should have spent your money on a nunnery rather than

Above
Left The glittering water chain.
Centre Water running through the central channel of the stone table was used to keep bottles cool during the Cardinal's banquets.
Right The twin casinos on the lower terrace, seen from the circular island of the Fountain of the Moors.

Opposite
Left Plan of the garden of the Villa Lante, from Percier and Fontaine, 1809.
Right In the Fountain of the Giants the colossal river gods of the Tiber and the Arno lie covered with moss.

squandering it on this garden.' At this time there was only one pavilion. Chastened, Gambara abandoned his plan to build a second and instead spent the money on building a hospital and repairing the cathedral of Viterbo. It would be another decade before a symmetrical twin of Palazzina Gambara was built by a later owner, Cardinal Alessandro Montalto.

The water comes to rest in four ponds in the Lake Garden, where four ferrymen are waiting to take passengers across the River Styx. In the central Fountain of the Moors, four muscular athletes lift Montalto's coat of arms, which is in the shape of mountains topped by a star. Originally the water was pushed up through the star and fell down in such a way as to obscure the four young men behind a thin, pyramid-shaped veil of water. This clever construction was the work of Tommaso Ghinucci from Siena, who was also responsible for the hydraulics at the Villa d'Este.

The terrace is split into twelve blocks, the outer eight consisting of parterres of box (*Buxus sempervirens*) and yew (*Taxus baccata*) punctuated by lemon trees in big urns. The garden used to be richer in plants: there were laurel hedges, supported by low trellises, with fruit trees at intervals; citrus trees, pomegranates and from the seventeenth century cherries as well. Ivy and vines, interwoven with jasmine, clematis and hops, climbed the walls. Today the parterres are gravelled and framed by yew and box hedges, perfectly clipped. The secret is revealed when the gardener points to a support inside one of the healthy, springy hedges. A clever frame, made from water-resistant bamboo and invisible from the outside, has been created for the yew.

'We don't get a frost very often but when we do, the garden is incredibly beautiful, even though snow is its worst enemy,' says Giovannino Fatica.

Water and ice. There is a snow tank from the sixteenth century in the ground near the old hunting lodge in the forest. It is a cylindrical ice-box, with a diameter of 10 metres (30 feet) and buried as deep. On 6 January 1601, a decision was taken to fill the tank with snow, at the expense of the town of Bagnaia, so that Cardinal Montalto would have ice to cool his drinks during the summer.

Many consider Villa Lante the most beautiful of all Italian Renaissance gardens. Most wonderful of all is the fact that so much of it is preserved as it was five hundred years ago.

Opposite The Lake Garden, with the Fountain of the Moors in the centre. Of the twelve blocks of the terrace the inner four are ponds, where ferrymen wait in their stone boats to take passengers across the River Styx. The outer eight are designed as parterres of box and yew.

ROSES, RUINS AND ROMANCE

CREATED BY THE CAETANI FAMILY IN THE TWENTIETH CENTURY

Giardino di Ninfa

Sermoneta

The history of Ninfa is like a fairy tale. Ruled from the beginning by popes, princes and princesses, what was once a prosperous town is today a twenty-acre garden, with fabulous magnolias, wisterias, irises, exotic trees and five hundred different types of rose. This garden paradise was created by the Caetani family, who were gifted Ninfa by Pope Boniface VIII in 1297.

I leave Rome by car and drive south along the Via Appia. Ninfa lies adjacent to the former Pontine Marshes. The region has expanded greatly since the 1930s, when Mussolini drained the marshes and reclaimed the land. Gradually the small factories by the side of the road are replaced by farmhouses and cultivated fields, and when the impressive escarpment of Monte Norma fills my windscreen I know I'm almost there. Ninfa is like an isolated island, a lost world that was reawakened in the twentieth century by the landowners, Prince Gelasio and his English mother, Ada Wilbraham. Their ambition was to create a romantic garden from the ruined town that had been left untouched for five hundred years.

Above A rose bush supported by the branch of a tree dips its pink petals in the water. No plastic or metal is to be found at Ninfa: all plant supports are those provided by nature.

Right A thousand years ago Ninfa was a flourishing town, a stopping place close to the Via Appia. The inhabitants earned a good living by levying tolls, providing travellers with hospitality and selling water to neighbouring communities.

Opposite
Top left In the castle tower of Ninfa next to the remains of the city wall covered in roses, there lives the blue bird, *Passero solitario*. In May, but no other month, she sings beautifully every morning at five o'clock.
Top right The handsome tree behind the Ponte del Macello was planted by Princess Ada Caetani to bring to Ninfa and her family 'luck and protection'.
Middle left Daffodils flourish in spring before the trees have burst into leaf.
Middle right White wisteria swathes the façade of the former city hall.
Bottom left A stream bordered by white arum lilies (*Zantedeschia aethiopica*) meanders through the garden.
Bottom right Miniature waterfalls mark changes of level along the stream.

In the nineteenth century, the German historian Gregorovius described Ninfa as a medieval Pompeii. At that time the remains of the buildings were overgrown by ivy, thorny blackberries and impenetrable wild vegetation. Today, under proper care, old-fashioned roses, ivy and honeysuckle cover the ruins. An air of magic remains, with tree trunks and rocks wrapped in a veil of romance and mystery.

The backdrop is like a theatrical scene, with the vine-covered town wall turning red every autumn, the hilltop town of Norma shrouded in mist almost all year round and the ruins of the old church of Santa Maria Maggiore with its faded frescoes in the chancel.

After only five minutes in the park I am filled with a great sense of peace. The sound of water and birdsong has a calming influence. Lauro Marchetti, who manages the park on behalf of the Roffredo Caetani Foundation, appears without a sound in a small battery-powered vehicle. The conservation area extends for more than twenty acres so he needs some means of getting around – and whatever transport he uses has to be environmentally friendly.

'Ninfa is the last oasis in this part of Italy,' says Lauro Marchetti quietly, 'not only because of the trees and plants, but equally because of the spiritual atmosphere, the birds and nature as a whole. What is so special about this place is that one can feel the genuine side of life. That is unusual today.'

The drama begins in February, after two months of winter rest. First to appear on the scene are the magnolias, their buds unfolding in pale pink and white. *Magnolia campbelli* from the Himalayas opens her petals first of all. It took her thirty years to flower for the first time, but now her blooms are richer each year. In April the cherry trees take over and Ninfa dons a stronger colour. The flowers of the ornamental cherry P*runus* 'Accolade' and of *P.* 'Ukon' and the bright pink apple *Malus purpurea* float gently in the air and the ground is covered in daisies and forsythias. During the long rose season, there is always at least one of the five hundred types in flower. At first I think that the end of April and beginning of May is definitely the best time to visit Ninfa, but after an autumn visit, in the beginning of November, I'm no longer sure. The air is clean and clear, and who can resist a river where the trees are reflected in red and yellow?

Behind the old town wall is a lake that supplies the park with water. From a subterranean spring clean water flows into the winding River Ninfa, which brings water

to every corner of the garden. I'm handed a mug made out of bamboo and I take a sip of the water. It tastes delicious, fresh and pure.

Of course, the garden doesn't look after itself (in case anyone thought so). No, the truth is that Ninfa has a small team of gardeners who weed, cut and fertilize all year round. It takes a lot of work to maintain the natural character of the garden; plants need a helping hand, for example, in finding a new route upwards around a tree trunk or a ruin. The ecological side is very important to Lauro Marchetti: the compost heaps that lie beautifully integrated in the shadiest parts of the garden are a great source of pride.

It feels eerie to wander around the ruins of this lost world, even in daylight when the garden is open. Ninfa's golden age lasted for six hundred years during the Middle Ages when, a small but rich town, she played an important role as a link between Rome and Naples. In Ninfa travellers could take a break, stay overnight, eat well and drink the best water in southern Italy. It was a comfortable existence for the twelve hundred inhabitants, who only had to collect the toll charges. During the twelfth century Ninfa was ruled by the Frangipani family who had several churches built, together with a city wall. After it came into the possession of the Caetani family in 1297, Ninfa reached the height of its success. In 1382, however, papal conflicts and family feuding resulted in Ninfa being attacked and sacked. It never recovered. Malaria had already begun to empty the medieval towns in the region and now war did the rest. Ninfa faded into oblivion and wild plants took root in the stonework of the slowly crumbling buildings.

We reach the wonderful river that meanders through the garden. Lauro squats down on the Ponte del Macello and beckons a family of ducks. To my surprise, the mother duck leaves her family and waddles up to Lauro, and a short 'conversation' takes place.

What is more important in a garden, I ask, health or beauty? Lauro takes a decisive step towards the compost heap and picks up a handful, staining his green linen suit.

'Natural is beautiful. Some plants suffer from parasites, but we have never been tempted to use chemicals. Instead we allow the plants to live through it. At the end of the disease the plant can still survive in balance with the birds and the insects. That is our goal. And if the soil is nutritious, the plants will be strong enough to combat the disease.'

It is important that the ecological system is in balance – only then is the park beautiful. Beauty and ecology go together.

Opposite Through all the seasons the river is a paradise. The banks are lined by flaming smoke tree (*Cotinus coggygria* 'Flame'), many species of magnolia, cherry trees including weeping cherry (*Prunus* 'Pendula Rosea') and wild cherry (*P. avium*) and *Wisteria floribunda* 'Macrobotrys'.

By the Roman bridge, the Japanese wisteria *W. floribunda* 'Macrobotrys' dips its long pink-purple racemes in the clear water. The flowers are at their most beautiful in April and May, but in November the plant displays an interesting network of strong branches. It will spend the next four months gathering strength before bursting into bloom again in April. Along the river we also find magnolias, cherries, camellias, mahonias and lilies.

When Gelasio Caetani died in 1935 his brother Roffredo inherited Ninfa, and together with his American wife Marguerite he expanded the park. In the 1940s Princess Marguerite started an international literary review, *Botteghe Oscure*, and she opened the park for the first time to special guests associated with the journal. They used to sit down to lunch under the trees and discuss literature. Their daughter Lelia Caetani, who was an artist, lived at Ninfa for over twenty years with her husband, Hubert Howard. They expanded the garden with the creation of arboreta and brought in many new types of trees and plants. Unfortunately there are few plant lists or garden plans left from this period, but Lelia's paintings remain as a testimony.

Lelia, the last member of the Caetani family, died in 1977, after the family had spent more than six hundred years at Ninfa. Ownership passed to the Roffredo Caetani

Foundation, with Lauro Marchetti assuming day-to-day responsibility. His mission in life had been decided long before. He used to play in the park as a little boy. When he was seven years old Lelia asked him if he wanted to stay at Ninfa. He replied:

'Yes, but for how long?'

'I think,' said Lelia, 'for the rest of your life.'

Lauro remembers that she was tall and beautiful . . .

'Ninfa is my destiny,' he says. 'Life threw me an opportunity and I took it. I can't change my life now.'

One year after the death of Lelia Caetani in 1977, Ninfa was opened to the public for the first time.

A new generation has come to Ninfa. The garden is involved in a school project; every year 22,000 pupils from Rome and Naples visit the park. The intention is not only that the children should enjoy the beautiful flowers but also that their understanding of conservation should be encouraged – to give them a first lesson in ecological responsibility. Guides conduct the visits and teachers are informed that it is not a holiday outing, but a lesson in how fragile nature is.

'When they arrive here they are usually rowdy, talk in loud voices and chew gum. But after ten minutes something happens; their behaviour changes without us having to tell them off. They absorb the atmosphere of the garden and become calm. I tear my hair out when we have a thousand pupils in the garden at the same time,' Lauro chuckles and adds: 'It is dangerous for Ninfa, but necessary.'

Trout originating in Africa and Sardinia swim in the river. They were introduced here more than a thousand years ago. It is hard to imagine that only a couple of miles downstream effluent from a factory is discharged into the water. Here the water is still safe to drink. A couple of years ago Lauro Marchetti led the fight against the establishment of a new factory in the area. The local population supported him.

Ninfa is owned and managed by a private foundation. Funds to sustain the garden and ruins come mainly from ticket sales, and from government grants.Today Ninfa enjoys the protection of the WorldWide Fund for Nature, whose symbol is displayed on the iron gate. Lauro's dream for the future is a bigger nature park, an expansion that would resist all attempts to create an industrial area and that would give the Italians a great ecological garden to visit. It is a dream that is in the process of coming true.

Opposite *Magnolia* x *soulangeana* 'Lennei' from the Himalaya frames the lake and the waterfall.

Above A bud of the magnolia about to open its beautiful pink petals in March.

WATER GARDEN IN THE MOUNTAINS
DESIGNED BY PIRRO LIGORIO AND TOMMASO GHINUCCI
FOR IPPOLITO II D'ESTE 1550–75

Villa d'Este

Tivoli

At Villa d'Este, perhaps the most perfect of all the High Renaissance gardens, the most characteristic feature is not the planting but the water, which cascades out of the spouts of the imaginative fountains and creates works of art in the air.

This country estate is to be found seventeen miles outside Rome, high on the western foothills of the Sabine mountains in the village of Tivoli. The moving spirit behind the garden was Ippolito II d'Este, Cardinal of Ferrara, who was appointed Governor of Tivoli in 1550. Ippolito was attracted by the lovely scenery, the clear air and the fact that there was plenty of water in the River Aniene 160 metres (525 feet) below. The area is also of great historical interest with many important relics from Roman times, including the ruins of Hadrian's Villa, built by the emperor in the second century AD.

The architect Isabella Barisi, who has been the Director of the Villa d'Este since 1995, shows me around. The estate is now owned by the Italian Government and it is listed by UNESCO as a World Heritage Site. Restoration work has been ongoing since the beginning of the new millennium, but according to Barisi a lot still remains to be done. For example, one of the richly decorated rooms, the Room of the Fountain, has a fresco depicting Villa d'Este in 1568, framed by an abundance of fruits. It is a magnificent painting, but the pigment has faded. Soon the restorers will have reached this area with their ladders and tools, and the colours of the frescoes will regain their intensity – for better or for worse.

'The Cardinal used the villa as his summer residence, the staterooms being on the ground floor and his private rooms above. He would arrive in June and stay until

Once again music can be heard from the newly restored water organ. The water cascades down a waterfall designed by Baroque artist Gian Lorenzo Bernini into the Fountain of Neptune before coming to rest in the three fishponds below.

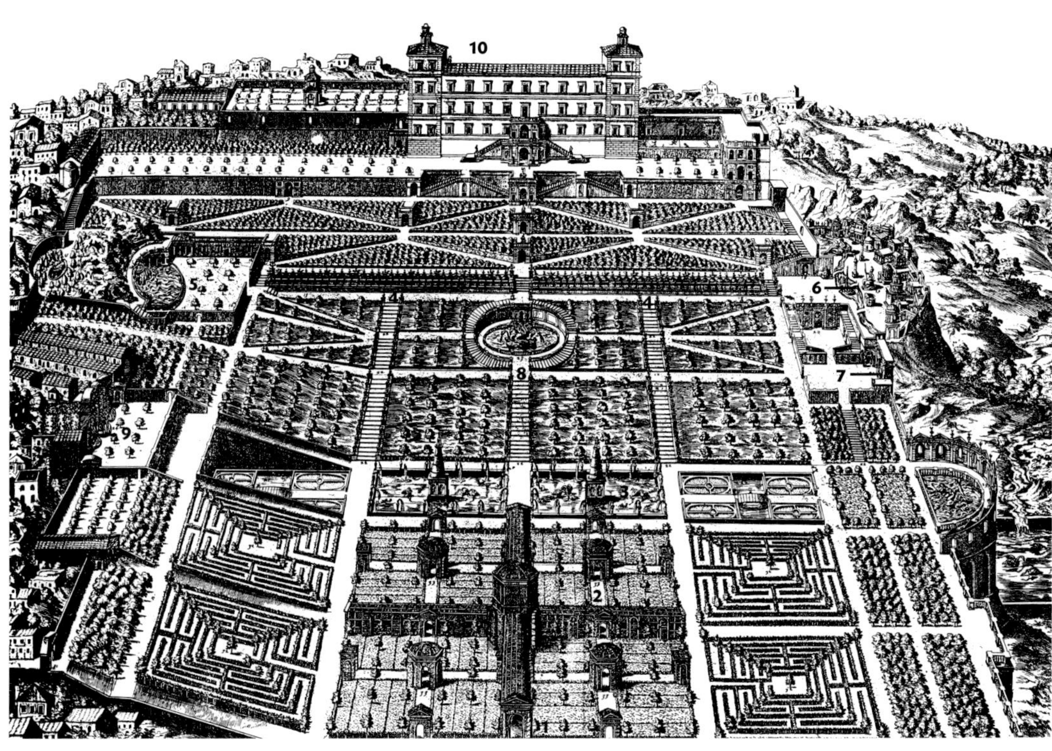

1 Historic entrance
2 Trellis and pavilion
3 Fishpools
4 Pathway of the Hundred Fountains
5 Oval Fountain
6 Rometta Fountain
7 Fountain of the Owl
8 Fountain of the Dragons
9 Water organ
10 Modern entrance

September or October. The palace and the garden face north-west, which is the cooler side. The water indoors was supposed to remind him of the fountains in the garden,' Isabella Barisi explains.

On our way out into the garden, we pause to have a quick espresso in the Italian fashion, *al banco* – standing by the counter in the cafeteria. From the terrace, the view across the Roman *campagna* is breathtaking. The village of Tivoli clings to the mountain in the north, two church spires can be seen in the distance, and in the west olive groves cover the slopes. In Roman times, vines were grown climbing up the olive trees. They were grapes of an unusual type called *pizzutello*, a name which accurately describes the long and pointed form.

Villa d'Este sends out conflicting signals. The stone, the dark green straight hedges and the perfect geometrical layout speak of power and formality. As a disarming contrast, the garden is filled with *giochi d'acqua*. These playful water jokes, characteristic of Renaissance gardens, are hidden in the most unexpected places to surprise unsuspecting guests, who are showered by water from hidden spouts in the ground, on stairs, all over the garden.

Cardinal Ippolito II d'Este saw no limits when designing the villa. He was rich and an art lover, and he wanted to see his fantasy come true. The difficult task of building a villa on a cliff side, based on examples from Antiquity, fell on the archaeologist and architect Pirro Ligorio. For Renaissance thinkers, the spirit of the place was very important, and Ligorio could sense the magic of nature in this spot. He saw the place in a larger context, linked to the imperial villas of Roman times. He had studied the ruins of Hadrian's Villa, and also the Lucullus Gardens above the Spanish Steps in

Opposite
Top left and *bottom right* The Pathway of the Hundred Fountains, with *giochi d'acqua* – water jokes – in every shape and form. Figures from Ovid's *Metamorphoses* can be glimpsed among the thick growth of maidenhair ferns.
Top right The beautiful Oval Fountain, with the statue of the Sibyl above the curtain of water.
Bottom left The three fishponds form the main cross-axis of the garden.

Above The gardens of the Villa d'Este as they were in 1573, in an etching by Du Pérac.

Top A grotesque figure from the Pathway of the Hundred Fountains.
Bottom The Fountain of the Dragons, shooting a jet of water high up into the air.

Rome. He made drawings of the Lucullus Gardens, which encapsulated the fundamental form which would later come to typify the Renaissance villas around Rome: a series of terraces on a slope, with stairs, ramps and a columned semicircular apse as a backdrop.

The garden is laid out along a main axis which starts at the gate in the city wall (by Via del Colle) and continues, passing the Fountain of the Dragons halfway, to the villa. The difference in ground levels from the highest to the lowest point was 50 metres (165 feet). The slopes had to be filled in and terraces created. Workers shifted boulders, moved soil and built enormous vaults and buttresses to support the terraces.

Today visitors enter the gardens from above, via the palace, but in the sixteenth century guests would have arrived through the entrance gate in the wall of the lowest level. They continued slowly through a wooden pergola, similar to those of Roman gardens, covered in fragrant jasmine, ivy and delicious grapes. Through the latticework, they would have glimpsed the palace far away on the hill. Soon they reached a small wooden trellised pavilion, crowned with a golden lily. Above them, the cupola was covered by roses, jasmine and ivy. The surrounding quadrangles were filled with small pomegranates and other fruit trees, within low hedges of rosemary, lavender, myrtle and box. Further on were the Cardinal's flower garden and a herb garden with medicinal plants for use by the household. In the seventeenth century, the wooden trellises were removed and replaced by a circle of cypresses: the Cypress Rotunda. Today, these cypresses no longer stand tall, but they are growing old with beauty and dignity, with silvery grey trunks and a bonsai-like knottiness. Their roots have to fight for nourishment, hindered by stones and the vaults which support the terraces.

Pirro Ligorio carried out archaeological excavations at Hadrian's Villa and brought several antique statues to Villa d'Este. According to travel diaries from the seventeenth century there used to be sixty groups of statues.

'The statues were bought in the eighteenth century by Englishmen. Later, when they were sold on, they ended up all over the world. Some of the statues can now be found in the Louvre, others in the museums of the Vatican. Some are in Galleria Borghese and several in the Capitoline Museums in Rome. It is my dream to be able to bring the statues back to Villa d'Este and to show them here,' says Isabella Barisi.

But the outstanding features of the Villa d'Este are the spectacular water displays created more than four hundred years ago by Tommaso Ghinucci from Siena. It is surprising to think that though little survives of the original system, the principles

Top The water in the Oval Fountain creates a semicircular curtain, veiling the walkway behind. *Bottom* The Rometta Fountain, by Pirro Ligorio, portrays the Seven Hills of Rome and major monuments including the statues of Rome Victorious and the She-Wolf Nursing the Twins, the Colosseum and the Pantheon.

remain the same. The hydraulic knowledge of the Romans had been developed further during the Renaissance, and water was brought to the villa in three ways: from the River Aniene via the Estense Canal built in 1563–65, from a restored Roman aqueduct that carried water from Monte Sant'Angelo, and by collecting rainwater in giant tanks. The water from the river is collected in a cistern immediately above the Oval Fountain. From here, gravity takes over and the water flows through ducts and pipes to the fountains at lower levels. A pump supplies the higher fountains with water. During the first hundred years, the pipes were usually made from clay or terracotta. Later they were replaced by leather pipes and later still by plastic.

In the Oval Fountain – perhaps the most beautiful of all the fountains in the garden – the water cascades from a projecting roof and creates a transparent semicircular curtain. Inside is a path wide enough to walk on. It is easy to imagine the Cardinal and his entourage in their long, sweeping clothes using this cooler detour on hot days. Above is a statue of the Sibyl, the oracle of classical Antiquity who was also seen as a Christian symbol. The Sibyl, surrounded by greenery, gazes towards the Rometta Fountain, which was shaped like a miniature Rome, as a reminder to visitors from the city that they must maintain high moral standards. Also on this level are the three rows of small fountains that make up the Pathway of the Hundred Fountains.

Water is also used to make music. At the Fountain of the Organ, I enter the engine room, where the machinery that creates the music is demonstrated. To put it briefly, it works by an interplay between water and air, and creates sounds via two separate pipes, whirlpools and a metal drum (which looks like a giant old-fashioned music box). It's a sophisticated system which was recently restored by Rodney Briscoe, an Englishman and one of the few people in the world who know this craft. The Fountain of the Organ plays music four to five times a day, every other hour, for around five to six minutes. Hearing the music mixed with the sound of the continuously flowing, tinkling water is an unforgettable experience.

After many years of silence, the Fountain of the Owl has also finally been restored. A group of man-made birds are singing in harmony before being frightened off by an owl. In a moment they are back, continuing their sweet-sounding songs. Below ground are several water spouts, *giochi d'acqua*, buried in the mosaics. At the reinauguration of the fountain in 2002 this system was switched on, and the jets surprised the press photographers, who were showered by water. The Cardinal would have been amused.

SECRET GARDENS
DESIGNED FOR SCIPIONE BORGHESE BY FLAMINIO PONZO 1608–13 AND JAN VAN SANTEN, KNOWN AS GIOVANNI VASANZIO
SUNDIAL GARDEN PROBABLY DESIGNED BY CARLO RAINALDI 1680S

The Old Garden, planted with pillows of santolina, salvia, lavender and other aromatic plants, with tall blue irises (*Iris germanica*) in between. Citrus trees in pots are mounted on pedestals, so that their scent wafts into the air at nose level.

Giardini Segreti of Villa Borghese

Rome

The Pincian Hill in Rome was once covered by vineyards, but in the seventeenth century it was transformed by Cardinal Scipione Borghese into a hunting and pleasure park, which was named Villa Borghese. Next to Casino di Villa Borghese, three *giardini segreti*, secret gardens, were laid out in a row.

Secret – in what way? The idea of the enclosed garden originated in Roman times and was developed further in the cloister garden, *hortus conclusus*, of the medieval period. In the villas and palaces of the Italy of the Renaissance and Baroque eras the *giardino segreto* was usually next to the house, forming a single unit enclosed by a tall wall or hedge. No uninvited person would be able to see or enter the owner's private paradise.

The secret gardens of Villa Borghese gave the Cardinal a place to withdraw and stroll with friends and colleagues. Maybe they discussed politics, philosophy and art, or talked about the rare tulip bulbs which commanded such vast sums of money in the early seventeenth century. The Cardinal wished above all for the garden to be fragrant. The flower beds were filled with herbs and aromatic plants which were thought to ward off disease. Citrus trees were placed on pedestals so that their scent would reach the nostrils of the Cardinal and his guests as they strolled past.

Since 1903 the Villa Borghese has been a public park. It is the most central of all the parks in Rome, and its green expanse is bordered by the meandering Via Veneto to the south-east, the residential Parioli area to the north, Piazza del Popolo to the west and the Spanish Steps to the south. The best way to reach the park is on foot, via the Spanish Steps, past Villa Medici, housing the French Academy, and then up the steps to the Pincian Hill. From here you have stunning views across Rome. Continue walking

past the spring-flowering cherries and almonds, the graceful plane trees and the gigantic pines along Piazza di Siena, and you will reach the secret gardens in the north-east corner of the park, beside Casino di Villa Borghese .

These *giardini segreti* have recently been reconstructed to an appearance as close as possible to the way they were when they were first created, in the seventeenth century. Seeing them is a unique way of getting an idea of what flower beds would have looked like between three and four hundred years ago. The restoration work was preceded by many years of research in the archives in Rome, studying historical documents. Garden historian and designer Ada Segre, who was consulted for the planning and horticultural design of the gardens, describes the sources: 'Detailed planting plans of gardens in Rome, plant lists exchanged among flower lovers, especially the Caetani and the Barberini families, illustrations of plants, treatises on horticulture, both published and in manuscript form, and letters between various flower connoisseurs. The

The birdcages of the Aviary Garden used to house exotic birds whose song entertained guests strolling in the garden. The flower beds, laid out in seventeenth-century style, are mainly planted with bulbs, including anemones, fritillaries, crocus, daffodils, agapanthus and tulips, with the addition of violets, feverfew and some more exotic plants. Lemon trees grow in tall pots.

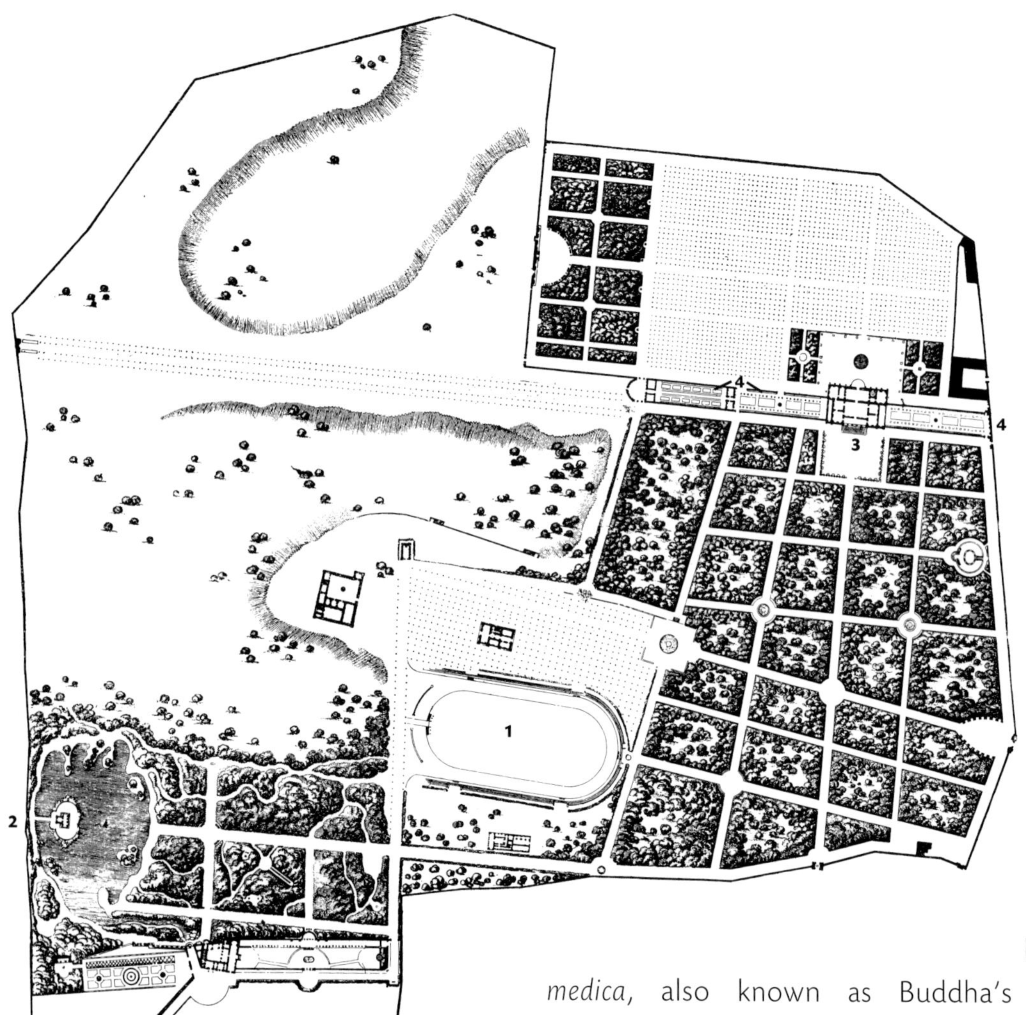

1 Piazza di Siena
2 Lake and Temple of Esculapius
3 Galleria Borghese
4 Giardini Segreti

documentary research undertaken by Alberta Campitelli at the Department of Historic Villas and Parks at Comune di Roma was particularly valuable.'

Ada and I take a walk around the three secret pleasure gardens. The first garden, to the right of Casino di Villa Borghese, is known as the Old Garden. During the seventeenth century, there were more than 140 citrus trees in terracotta pots, lined up in twenty-four rows. Today, the numbers are considerably less. An unusually knobbly lemon draws my attention. It looks like a hand with long fingers and it is the *Citrus medica*, also known as Buddha's hand. According to Claudia Lazzaro's *The Italian Renaissance Garden*, the sweet types of orange were common in Italy in the mid-sixteenth century, together with lemons, quinces, peaches, pears, plums, cherries and apricots. The large ovoid lemon species *Citrus medica* was very popular, despite its acid flesh and hard, strong-smelling rind.

There are also lemons from the Salerno area, and another variety from southern Italy, which is used for making the famous Limoncello lemon liqueur. During the winter, the tender citrus trees are kept in glasshouses. In the small flower beds there are several varieties of iris, among them the yellow *Iris germanica.* Their leaves are spear-shaped and create interesting vertical lines in the garden. Aromatic herbs include lemon balm, sage, cotton lavender and large cushions of cress. Orange marigolds are combined, rather unusually, with grass. The flower beds on the far left are filled with roses of the species *gallica, damascena, centifolia* and *alba.* The cultivars were chosen from ancient varieties such as *Rosa gallica* 'Versicolor' and *R. alba*. Or they were chosen because they were reminiscent of the old-fashioned varieties, for example *R.* 'Belle Amour'. The scents combine in a perfume which is not intense but rather a faint, secret fragrance which creeps up on you like a breath of air.

'Scent was the key to the aesthetic appreciation of gardens during the seventeenth century,' says Ada. 'The plants were divided into groups depending on appearance and

scent. The first group consisted of plants with scented flowers. The second group was not eye-catching but the whole plant was fragrant. The idea was that diseases came with the pollution of the air; the scent was thought to protect against disease.'

Secret garden number two, the Aviary Garden, is on the other side of the Casino di Villa Borghese. On the garden pavilion there are birdcages, almost like airy towers. Imagine how the songbirds would have been competing with each other, one singing more beautifully than the other, despite a life in captivity. The building is superbly decorated with antique sculptures in relief and the family coat of arms. The flower beds contain a rich variety of the bulbous plants such as anemones, hyacinths, narcissi and, of course, tulips, which were so highly prized in the sixteenth and seventeenth centuries.

The third garden is the Sundial Garden, which gets its name from a large sundial there. The casino building was designed by Carlo Rainaldi and Tommaso Mattei about 1680–83. Rainaldi was in all probability the architect of this third secret garden, but the evidence is not conclusive. As in the other gardens, the wall is lined with citrus trees. The flower beds are divided into patterns by sandy paths, the light-coloured sand providing a nice contrast to the dark soil and the abundance of flowers. In the middle of the garden is a star-shaped flower bed. A large terracotta pot holds a flowering yucca, one of many exotic plants introduced to Italy over the centuries.

The garden at the far end is now used as a nursery for the other three.

Having once been a hunting ground for cardinals, Villa Borghese is now a popular park, playing host to many different activities. The Casino di Villa Borghese is an art gallery, Galleria Borghese, holding the Scipione Borghese Collection of Classical, Renaissance and Baroque Art. At Piazza di Siena, an international horse show takes place every year. There are also zoological gardens with more than a thousand animals. Outside the gate, in a north-western direction, is the Etruscan Museum in the sixteenth-century Villa Giulia. The villa has an historical garden with a nymphaeum designed by Vignola in 1550; the arcade and vault are decorated with beautiful paintings depicting trellises covered with grapes.

Top to bottom The lemon *Citrus medica,* known as Buddha's hand; iris leaves braided in seventeenth-century fashion, to keep them neat as they die back after flowering; ranunculus, introduced into European gardens in the sixteenth century; *Crocus sieberi.*

MONSTERS IN THE SACRO BOSCO

DESIGNED BY PIRRO LIGORIO FOR VICINO ORSINI FROM 1552

Opposite The giant stone head known as the Mouth of Hell.

Below The crenellated entrance to Sacro Bosco, set in the mountainous landscape of the Lazio.

Sacro Bosco

Bomarzo

Sacro Bosco, Villa Orsini's enchanted forest below the village of Bomarzo, is at its most impressive in the morning mist or autumnal moonlight, when the outlines of the gigantic stone figures are blurred and you can only just make out the frightening creatures looming large among the trees and bushes.

Sacro Bosco spent several centuries in a deep sleep before being rediscovered at the beginning of the twentieth century. It was then a wooded area full of greenery and moss, with massive figures carved into rocks, overgrown by brushwood and roots which had broken through the forest floor. It must have been a surreal sight! There are sleeping nymphs on a giant scale, a tilting house, three-headed dogs and other mythological creatures. It is not hard to understand why the park had such an influence on many twentieth-century artists, among them Salvador Dalí.

Today I am experiencing the garden in neither mist nor moonlight, but early-morning sun that dapples down through the tree canopy. After passing through the elegant entrance gate, I am greeted by flowering cherries, apple trees in bud and Sphinxes – females with animal bodies. There is a perplexing inscription on one of the plinths: 'He who does not go there with eyes wide open and lips sealed will not be able to admire the most wonderful marvels.' Continuing, I come to a fork in the way. I am drawn to the path on the right, which leads down to the ravine. It could turn out to be a fatal decision. At the top of the steps, I stop in front of two giants engaged in a vicious fight. There are different theories about the identity of these figures. According to one version, Hercules is holding Cacus upside down, in a battle between good and evil. In another, Orlando

Above left The battle between Hercules and Cacus (or Orlando and the woodcutter).

Above right The winged horse Pegasus is a symbol of the Farnese family. The tortoise acts as a reminder of the value of progressing slowly and with due consideration.

(of Ludovico Ariosto's poem *Orlando Furioso*) is holding the woodcutter upside down, symbolizing the human struggle on the path to self-fulfilment. I notice that Cacus/the woodcutter is supporting himself by pressing his enormous foot – more than 1 metre (3 feet) long – against the wall, and then my eyes move over towards the swirling, magical waterfall opposite. Further along the ravine is a group of mythological creatures, with the winged horse Pegasus in the foreground. Pegasus has many symbolic meanings, but here in Sacro Bosco he is a symbol of the Farnese family. The tortoise at the far end can be seen as a reminder not to rush things. 'To the one who knows how to go slowly, fortune will display its glory,' says the inscription.

The enchanted forest of Bomarzo was created in the sixteenth century by Prince Vicino Orsini, who had lost his beloved wife, Giulia Farnese. The prince threw himself into the creation of Sacro Bosco as a way of soothing his broken heart – but also because he wanted a spectacular garden as a status symbol for the Orsini family. The prince decided to place his garden in the valley below the Orsini palace at Bomarzo. He sought help from the multi-talented architect Pirro Ligorio, who was also the architect of Villa d'Este (see page 34) and of Villa Pia in the Vatican palace gardens, one of the earliest and most perfect examples of a garden pavilion. In his 1553 book *Roman Antiquities*, Ligorio states that an architect should not only know how to draw and paint, he should also 'defend the arts and be knowledgeable about philosophy, the theory of music, symmetry, mathematics, astronomy, history, typography and the laws of perspective.' However, Ligorio had no need of his knowledge of symmetry when he created the monster garden of Bomarzo, with its statues and bizarre architecture scattered here and there among the trees.

Continuing my walk, I come across a niche in the rock with carvings of the Three Graces. The three young nymphs symbolize purity, and Pirro Ligorio probably had his three daughters Rosa, Chiara and Lucrezia in mind. Venus of Cimini stands in a shell,

Above left Ceres, goddess of the harvest, is a monumental presence among the greenery and mosses.

Above right A warrior elephant holds a soldier in his trunk.

and she ensures the fertility of the garden. The top part of the garden is reached via steps, which take you past the crooked house. What an absurd idea, to use a leaning rock to build a house! Signor Ligorio really did make full use of his imagination. On the top terrace, an elegant giantess sits on the ground. It is the goddess Ceres, balancing a bread-basket on her beautiful head. I try to take her picture between two tree trunks, but the shadows prevent me from doing her justice. A bit further along is the elephant – the wisest of all the animals, according to Ligorio, and also a symbol of Rome's victories and defeats. Why he carries a Roman legionary soldier in his trunk is anyone's guess.

Sacro Bosco is a puzzle. It is frequently described as a labyrinth where symbolic meanings can be discovered or as an enchanted forest representing the secrets of nature and the spiritual world that man has to enter to discover the meaning of life. Maybe I could get closer to solving the mystery by reading *Hypnerotomachia Poliphili* (*The Strife of Love in a Dream*), the famous work by the Dominican monk Francesco Colonna, first published in 1499. The creators of the Italian Renaissance gardens were influenced by Colonna's allegorical texts and the characters he created. The monster garden at Bomarzo is one of the best examples of Mannerism, an art form in which the artists tested their limits, and were braver and more playful than ever before. They felt that any work of art, regardless of whether it was a painting, a sculpture or a garden, should stir the emotions. It should make the viewer laugh, cry with fear or just stare in amazement at something totally absurd or bizarre.

It must have been an astonishing experience to come across the Sacred Forest and gradually watch the figures appear from beneath the layers of moss and lichen. Maybe Sacro Bosco will one day be overgrown again. I leave the forest behind, enriched by the experience but with just as many unanswered questions as before. The conundrum of Bomarzo remains unsolved, and maybe that is how it should be.

GARDEN ROOMS IN A COUNTRY ESTATE
CREATED BY LAVINIA TAVERNA GALLARATI SCOTTI 1950S–80S
WITH RUSSELL PAGE FROM 1967

Giardini della Landriana

Tor San Lorenzo

At the charming country estate of Landriana in Tor San Lorenzo, south of Rome, the gardens are in flower all year round. In spring, the bulbs, the magnolias and not least the glorious Apple Garden are at their best. Later on, the roses come into their own, and there is a slope covered in a spectacular sea of orangey pink *Rosa chinensis* 'Mutabilis'.

Landriana is situated in what used to be the Pontine Marshes, only about three miles from the Mediterranean. The owners, the Gallarati Scotti family, bought the farmland at an auction in the late 1950s. At that time the estate consisted of a simple farmhouse, pastures and a few stone pines. The Marchesa Lavinia Taverna Gallarati Scotti's first planting was a large collection of perennials, roses and succulents. They were mixed together in a fairly jumbled border, and she soon realized that if she was to create a coherent and beautiful garden she would need professional help. She turned to landscape architect Russell Page, who began designing the garden in 1967. The way the garden looks today is the result of their collaboration. Page was responsible for the overall plan, Lavinia for colour and detailed structure.

Top left The romantic lake, which was constructed in the 1980s.
Top right In the Orange Garden, Norway maples (*Acer platanoides* 'Globosum') and small bitter orange trees (*Citrus aurantium*) are planted in a repeated geometrical pattern. Spheres of clipped myrtle (*Myrtus communis*) flank the paths and creeping Jenny (*Lysimachia nummularia*) provides ground cover.
Bottom right Russell Page's subtle border of silvery grey Mediterranean plants has been moved from beside the house to near the garden entrance.
Bottom left The Yellow Border, from the house. The planting includes honey locust (*Gleditsia triacanthos* 'Sunburst'), honeysuckle (*Lonicera nitida* 'Baggesen's Gold'), Chinese lantern (*Abutilon megapotamicum*) and different varieties of *Coprosma*. Behind are laurustinus (*Viburnum tinus*), golden variegated holly (*Ilex aquifolium* 'Aurea Marginata'), coastal daisy bush (*Olearia solandri*) and false holly (*Osmanthus heterophyllus* 'Goshiki').

In the book *Russell Page: Ritratti di Giardini Italiani* (1998), Lavinia described how their first project was born: 'It didn't exactly come about in a traditional way with an architect coming to inspect a garden and then drawing up plans. The ideas came gradually as Russell walked around in the garden. He would say "here we could do this and that", then we talked for a bit and he gave me a rough idea of the main things that needed doing and a lot of advice to follow until his next visit . . . He always said that using measurements which are divisible by three makes things easier. A path should be 90 centimetres (3 feet) wide, a border 3 metres (12 feet), etc. Russell believed measurements divisible by three to be more harmonious.'

Page suggested the creation of the two garden rooms which are known today as the Olive Garden and the Orange Garden. The Olive Garden was where Lavinia's collection of plants would find a new home. In her book *La Compagnia di un Giardino* Lavinia described Russell Page's 'very special' way of planting: 'He chose not to plant in rows, but instead put different species in groups, evenly across the whole area. This meant that the effect was that of a large Oriental carpet, where colours were repeated in many places at regular intervals throughout the whole planting area.'

The Olive Garden was framed by cypresses, which Page later asked Lavinia to prune low so as to create vistas between the gardens. The planting is composed of lilacs, mauves and yellows against a background of the green and silvery grey foliage of the olive trees. In early April, yellow and white tulips are showing signs of life. A little later, they are joined by the tall orbs of *Allium rosenbachianum*. There are ground-covering yellow archangel (*Lamium galeobdolon*), irises and ancient medicinal herbs, such as rue (*Ruta graveolens*) with its buttery-yellow flowers, a bushy bronze-coloured fennel, southernwood (*Artemisia abrotanum*) and wormwood (*A. absinthium*).

In May, yellow roses come into flower and appear to stunning effect against a backdrop of faded allium orbs. It is something of a miracle that such a rich flowering garden can survive in this hot, dry environment. Director Alessandra Vinciguerra, who has been responsible for the gardens of Landriana since 1999, is kept constantly busy making sure all the plants are happy: 'Many plants die through lack of water. It is difficult to adjust the irrigation exactly for each room. Irises, which need a certain amount of moisture, won't survive underneath the olive trees, which prefer a dry climate. I may eventually turn the olive garden into a kitchen garden with grey- and green-leaved herbs.'

Opposite
Top left *Rosa chinensis* 'Mutabilis' with the Indian bead tree (*Melia azedarach*) in the Valley of Mutabilis Roses.
Top right In the Olive Garden, purple ornamental onion (*Allium rosenbachianum*) floats above beds of cotton lavender, fennel and sage.
Bottom right The Italian Garden: magnolias surround a pattern of interconnecting squares and oblongs formed by hedges of bay laurel. Purple *Verbena peruviana* provides ground cover.
Bottom left The White Walk, flanked by white and pale pink plants including lilies, iberis, hibiscus, *Rosa* 'Penelope' and *Salvia leucantha*.

Above Seville orange (*Citrus aurantium*) in the Orange Garden.

Opposite *Rosa glauca* in the Valley of Old Roses. Hundreds of roses grow on the slopes down to the lake.

In the Orange Garden, orange trees and maples (*Acer platanoides* 'Globosum') are arranged in a repeated geometrical pattern. Spheres of clipped myrtle flank the paths.

During his second visit, Russell Page suggested creating the White Walk – a long series of shallow steps flanked by white and pale pink perennials, climbing and shrub roses, fronted by iberis, thrift and sage. It is a delight to climb the long flight of steps slowly, enjoying the scents, before turning into the Italian Garden. This formal green garden room is one of Page's most famous designs. Made up of laurel hedges arranged in a pattern of interacting squares and oblongs, it is surrounded by southern magnolias (*Magnolia grandiflora*) and simply planted with pinky purple ground-covering Peruvian verbena (*Verbena peruviana*).

Lavinia continued to enlarge the garden after Page's death in 1985, indeed until she herself died in the late 1980s. The Valley of Old Roses, the largest garden room, slopes down towards the lake. The slope is covered in roses, growing in a carpet of thyme, lavender, nepeta and other perennials, and softly separated by grassy paths. The current owners, Lavinia's daughters, are considering enlarging the garden and creating a path around the lake.

From the lake, a flight of steps leads through the woods up to the Apple Garden, a shady hill flanked by bear's breeches (*Acanthus mollis*) and other plants with different types of foliage. During April, the flowering trees are so beautiful that you might think you have entered the Garden of Eden. At that time of year, the ground is covered in violas and tiny Mexican daisies (*Erigeron karvinskianus*).

During Lavinia's last years, she often sat – frail from illness – in a wicker chair on the charming verandah of the house and looked out towards the Yellow Border, a mixture of roses, climbers and other flowers of her favourite colour.

On my way out through the gate, I pass a crooked carob tree (*Ceratonia siliqua*). The tree comes from Sicily and was a gift from Lavinia's father when they bought the estate in 1958. It is past its prime now, and looks a bit sad, but it is still there.

CASINO GARDEN

Overall Design by Giacomo Barozzi da Vignola for Alessandro II Farnese from 1547

Above A bridge leads from the palace to the two symmetrical gardens, each divided by paths into four large quadrangles.

Opposite In front of the blue casino, two river gods flank a giant urn of bubbling water. Beneath them, water cascades down an elaborate staircase, to tumble from the mouth of a monster into a shell-shaped basin.

Villa Farnese

Caprarola

Entering the village of Caprarola from the main road is a strange experience. At the far end of the steep village street is the vast, light-coloured pentagonal Villa Farnese, built in the mid-sixteenth century by Cardinal Alessandro II Farnese, who transformed an old fortress into a pleasure palace with adjoining gardens. Among the most famous of the papal power houses, Villa Farnese is huge out of all proportion compared to the tiny village and the unassuming medieval houses along the main road and in the little alleyways.

The architect Giacomo Barozzi da Vignola designed the palace and the gardens as a symmetrical unit. The gardens are at the back of the palace, and to get there you have to pass through the building. The absolute symmetry at Villa Farnese is evident if you study a plan. Twin staircases lead up to the entrance. The paved front courtyard was once used by visitors arriving in their horse-drawn carriages, before they were taken to the inner courtyard where they could alight safely inside the palace walls. The spiral staircase is a work of art in its own right, with painted walls and double columns. The decorations are motifs from the lives of the Farnese family. The views across the village and the undulating landscape from the main windows give you some idea of what the family once owned: houses, churches, woodland and farmland. Having passed through the Map Room (*Sala del Mappamondo*) and the State Rooms, you reach the living quarters – two identical, symmetrical suites, with views across the formal gardens from the master bedrooms. One suite was for the honoured guest, the other for the host himself.

Crossing the bridge over the drained moat, you reach the two formal gardens. One faces north-east, the other south-west – one for summer and one for winter. Each is composed of four large quadrangles, divided by paths forming a cross.

On the second terrace of the Casino Garden are Bernini's Whispering Herms, carrying vases on their heads. Some have the Farnese symbol, a lily, carved into the stone.

During the sixteenth century the box hedge patterns would have been filled with flowers.

But we won't stop here for long; instead we take a stroll through the surrounding woods, past junipers, oaks, pines and chestnuts. The air is high and clear, sunlight is dappling through the foliage and the trees provide shade. Alessandro Farnese called this garden his *parchetto*, or 'little park'. In spring, the ground is covered in violas, anemones and other early flowers. A small house comes into view at the far end; it's like a miniature version of the large palace – a casino. This part of the estate, the Casino Garden, consists of terraced gardens. It was mainly laid out in the first decades of the seventeenth century for Cardinal Odoardo Farnese and was seen as a pleasure garden, *hortus delicarium*, from the Latin *delicium,* which means delight or sensual pleasure. It was meant to be a haven, to which the family could retreat to enjoy life in privacy, only a short stroll from the official life at the palace. They also had their own outdoor dining area here. The water comes from an oval-shaped pond where two river gods are resting. It dances and swirls down a beautiful water staircase and glitters just as it does in the gardens of Villa Lante (see page 20). Water is an integral feature in most gardens in the water-rich Cimini mountains. At the bottom is an oval pond which collects the water, and then jets it high into the air. The casino has at times been used as a summer holiday home by the president of the Italian republic, and as a result it has been difficult to get a chance to see this gem, hidden in the woods. On the second terrace are the Whispering Herms, standing in a row with urns on their heads in front of perfectly clipped box hedges, planted in patterns. The herms were created in the early seventeenth century by Pietro Bernini at the request of Girolamo Rainaldi. Odoardo Farnese's will, dating from 1626, mentions that the garden had fifty-five fruit trees in giant urns, myrtle clipped into peacock shapes and ten urns with myrtle forming the coat of arms of the Farnese family. On the stone railings leading up to the top terrace, water comes out of the mouths of dolphins and falls into shells. It is in every respect a garden for a prince-cardinal.

THE OTTAVIA ORSINI PARTERRE

Southern Part of Garden Designed by Giacomo Barozzi da Vignola for Ottavia Orsini from 1611

Parterre possibly Designed by Ottavia Orsini 1611

Castello Ruspoli

Vignanello

Ottavia Orsini's initials, OO, were worked into the box parterres of the Greenery Garden, created at Castello Ruspoli during her stewardship in the early seventeenth century.

The narrow road through the village of Vignanello turns sharply left next to a small open space. Straight ahead Castello Ruspoli dominates the village, but there is nothing on the outside to suggest that Italy's most famous box parterre, and one of Europe's oldest, is hidden behind the thick walls.

Castello Ruspoli is very impressive but, with its anonymous grey stone façade, also a little bit frightening. There is a drawbridge with heavy chains, and the family coat of arms sits above the entrance. The castle has four defensive bastions, one in each corner, and a deep dry moat. When the gate opens there is a hint of something shimmering green far away on the other side – the garden.

Benedictine monks built the original fortress in the middle of the village, in the ninth century. For hundreds of years they managed to defend themselves against enemies. But by the sixteenth century there was no longer any need for a defensive structure, and the medieval castle was transformed into a fortified residential palace. The plans were probably drawn up by architect Antonio da Sangallo the Younger, in 1531, at the request of the owner, Alfonso Marescotti. In 1574, Count Marcantonio Marescotti of Vignanello married Ottavia Orsini, the daughter of Vicino Orsini who created the garden of Bomarzo (see page 44). After the death of her husband Ottavia took over the responsibility for the family estate, as their sons were not yet of age.

Ottavia, a wise and intelligent woman who had grown up in a cultured family, lived in an era when the ideas and ideals of the

The historic garden parterre is laid out on a terrace. From above, the patterns forming the initials of Ottavia and her sons Sforza and Galeazzo can clearly be seen. The letters F and R stand for Francesco Ruspoli.

Renaissance had a huge influence on the aristocracy, and these ideas are reflected in the garden she made. The castle had already been transformed into a Renaissance palace, and within the walls she had the ground and the steep slopes turned into a large flat terrace. A new gate was added on the eastern side and a bridge was built across the moat, so that the new area could be easily reached. The entire complex was framed by a wall and chestnut trees. In 1611 Ottavia had a parterre made up of clipped mixed hedges forming decorative patterns laid out on the terrace.

The parterres are divided by five transverse axes and two main axes, which draw the eye out into the surrounding landscape. In front of the parterres there is an orchard and some woodland; today this area is occasionally used for concerts.

The family can relax on the shady terrace, surrounded by hydrangeas in crackled terracotta pots.

Parterres are best viewed from above. Having struggled up the steep stairs, past old military lances decorating the walls, we reach the fourth floor of Castello Ruspoli. Down below, the parterre is spread out like a carpet. Made up of twelve rectangular compartments, their patterns emphasized by the surrounding sand, it looks almost like a mathematical formula.

The head gardener, Santino, is busy pruning the box with a scythe-like, crescent-shaped very sharp knife, which in Italian is known as a *falcetto*. He is shaping the two O's for Ottavia Orsini, which are repeated in several compartments. The compartment in front of the house contains the initials of her two sons, Sforza and Galeazzo, with the upside-down S and G perfectly joined together to form a pattern. We don't know who drew up the plans for the parterre, but since Ottavia signed her garden almost like a work of art, it seems reasonable to assume that it may have been Ottavia herself.

The box hedges are trimmed twice a year. This work takes Santino a couple of weeks each time. Castello Ruspoli received financial support from the EU in 1999 and the parterres have been completely overhauled and restored. They are definitely an important part of Europe's cultural heritage.

On the right-hand side of the estate is the small *giardino segreto* – the secret garden. It is sunken and made up of low box hedges forming patterns: rectangles, circles, triangles and even a heart. A small cave carved into the rock was probably used as an outdoor dining area on hot summer days. Roses are climbing the rocky walls.

In the eighteenth century, the Marescotti and Ruspoli dynasties were united by marriage. Two sisters, Claudia and Giada Ruspoli, today own the estate of Castello Ruspoli. As Princess Giada lives in South America, it is mainly her sister, Princess Claudia, who looks after the palace and the garden. Apart from being responsible for the running of the estate, she is making plans for the future. One idea is to turn a part of the secret garden into a restaurant or an open-air theatre. While waiting for the financial resources to be sorted out, she shows visitors around the estate. It is often Claudia who sits, surrounded by her beloved Alsatians, just inside the entrance, selling the tickets.

A PASSION FOR TREES

Created by Russell Page in Collaboration with Donato Sanminiatelli from 1964

San Liberato

Bracciano

To the sound of jazz I stroll around the harmonious garden of San Liberato just above Lake Bracciano, north of Rome. Andrea Sanminiatelli Odescalchi, a member of the family that owns the estate, has taken a break and is playing his saxophone. The tones of jazz escape through the window above the small church, built in the fourth century and restored in the ninth. This ancient church is the only building left of the old Roman market town that once stood here.

San Liberato sits high on a mountain with views across the circular volcanic Lake Bracciano. Fifty years ago the only way of getting up the steep hill was by horse and cart. The lake is now a popular resort for people living in Rome and the Lazio. Far away across the water the picturesque village of Anguillara clings to the hillside. In the foreground the white sails of small leisure boats are vivid against the dark blue water. In the town of Bracciano the fairy-tale Castello Odescalchi, still owned by the descendants of the papal family who built it, towers above everything else. The family also owns the country estate of San Liberato, surrounded by chestnut woods, olive trees and farmland.

Andrea's father was the art historian Count Donato Sanminiatelli, who was married to Maria, née Odescalchi. When they came to San Liberato as newly weds in 1961 they both fell in love with the place and decided they would build a house here, and make a garden. Donato had a great enthusiasm for botany, especially for trees, and he immediately set to work on his own, laying out the first terraces and a large lawn in front of the house. But after a while he realized that he would need help to create the unique garden he wanted. He was determined to hire the best landscape architect, and after a lot of research he chose Russell Page, who at the time was working on the landscape garden of Villa Perosa in Turin. Russell Page also designed the gardens of La Landriana and La Mortella (see pages 48 and 74).

From the summerhouse there are views across Lake Bracciano through the foliage of the beautiful trees. If the weather turns cold, as it usually does in November, the trees and shrubs take on stunning autumnal shades of red, orange and yellow. In the foreground is a silver maple (*Acer saccharinum*).

When Page arrived at San Liberato in 1964 he was immediately fascinated by what he saw. He talked with excitement about 'something radioactive in the soil stimulating the vegetation in a remarkable way'. Lake Bracciano is an extinct volcano and the ground is therefore full of nutritious minerals. Trees can grow more than 1 metre (3 feet) in a year. Page's aim was to integrate the garden park into the surrounding landscape and to combine the family's interest in Mediterranean plants with the principles that lie behind the English tradition of garden-making. With this in mind he and Donato Sanminiatelli entered into a collaboration.

Andrea, the son of Donato and Maria, remembers the garden from his childhood in the 1960s: 'When I was a child, the trees were no more than a metre high. Russell planted things very densely. He wanted to see the results soon, preferably after five or six years. No one could believe their eyes when they came here. How could such a young garden have such tall trees and such large plants?'

The garden is laid out as an English landscape garden with a dominating sloping lawn. The land is surrounded by a chestnut wood, and the basic layout is often described as that of an amphitheatre, with the wood embracing the garden in a semicircle. To understand the principles behind it, you have to start with the three main vistas. From the house, the first one is towards the glittering water of Lake Bracciano, which is just visible by a weeping rosebud cherry (*Prunus subhirtella* 'Pendula'). It's like a secret opening, hidden from the outside. The second imaginary line leads your eyes to the groups of trees, where you can experience the colours of the changing seasons according to a carefully orchestrated plan. The avenue of magnolias defines a third vista, towards the wood, and links tamed nature with wild. If you follow the light to the end of the tunnel, the path

takes you past a thicket of bamboos, azaleas, camellias and large-leaved hydrangeas – *H. macrophylla* 'Blue Wave' and *H. aspera* ssp. *sargentiana* – with large, plump flowers which, because of the high level of iron in the soil, are an intense shade of blue.

The garden is divided into rooms with different themes, including the Rose Garden, the Perennial Border, the Herb Garden and the four Tree Zones. The garden was laid out with the church as a natural starting point. Next to the church is a herb garden with narrow paths and low hedge plants including abelias, mock orange (*Pittosporum tobira*), rock roses (*Cistus monspeliensis*, *C. incanus* and *C. albidus*) and Jerusalem sage (*Phlomis fruticosa*). The remarkable collection of ceanothus, flowering in many shades of blue from spring through to autumn, is not to be missed. A grey garden room with small compartments is reminiscent of a cloister garden. The old, knotty olive trees in the midst of the silvery foliage have pale pink roses climbing up their trunks. The beds are planted with lavenders (*Lavandula angustifolia* 'Hidcote') and cotton lavender (*Santolina chamaecyparissus*), as well as wormwood (*Artemisia*) and various sages.

The house was built at the far end of the land, blending in with the surrounding landscape. It was meant to give the impression that it had been there for ever. The façade is now covered in jasmines and climbing roses. The sound of water from the Stone Fountain can be heard at a distance. In front of the house, a pool is hidden behind a clipped laurel hedge. The path to the Pool House is flanked by the white rose 'Iceberg', a great favourite with Russell Page. The changing seasons can be viewed from the verandah. The climax is reached at the end of November or beginning of December, when the leaves turn many hues of red, yellow and orange.

San Liberato is an arboretum and the trees have been carefully selected according to their shape, colour or type of bark. I am here in December, to photograph the autumn colours and also to study the ancient ginkgo tree. *Ginkgo biloba* has finally turned yellow after a warm autumn. Andrea Sanminiatelli wants everything to be perfect and is worried because the trees did not acquire their autumn colours in November: 'I'm only completely satisfied if all the trees get their autumnal colours simultaneously.This year the maples, as well as the Kashmir cypresses [*Cupressus cashmeriana*] and snowy mespilus [*Amelanchier canadensis*], lost all their leaves before the gingko even turned yellow. Something is wrong, it's far too warm.'

The sugar maple (*Acer saccharum*) has intensely red leaves, as also has *Amelanchier canadensis*. The wind is sighing delightfully in the trees and I drag my feet slowly through

Opposite
Top left Maidenhair trees (*Ginkgo biloba*) glow gold in late autumn.
Top right An autumnal still life of Japanese maples, pampas grass with silvery plumes, sweet gum (*Liquidambar styraciflua*) and the ancient maidenhair tree.
Bottom left and right Japanese and red maples (*Acer palmatum* 'Dissectum' and *A. rubrum*).

the heaps of red, shiny, spear-like leaves from a black gum (*Nyssa sylvatica*). The tall sweet gum (*Liquidambar styraciflua*) looks like a maple but has more delicate, laciniated leaves and small spiny cones. Page liked the fact that there was a lot of space at San Liberato, which enabled him to plant species of trees which can grow very large. When he returned after fifteen years, he noted that the tulip tree (*Liriodendron tulipifera*), which was 1 metre (3 feet) high when it was planted in 1964, had grown to a height of 20 metres (65 feet).

Passing a camphor tree I pick up a leaf from the ground and crush it between my fingers. It smells wonderful. Suddenly there is a noise among the trees and a family of roe deer – eight, no, ten, eleven . . . twelve! of them – run past on the other side of the fence. A large, solid redwood looks as if it is close to two hundred years old, but turns out to be a mere twenty-seven. All over the garden, there are magnolias: *Magnolia denudata*, *M. stellata, M. sargentiana* 'Robusta', *M. soulangeana* and *M. fuscata*. A handkerchief tree (*Davidia involucrata)* has small fluttery leaves which protect the flowers. Page loved the Swedish cut-leaf weeping birch (*Betula pendula* 'Dalecarlica'), but it looks a bit sad as it has less water than it would in its natural environment.

'In August, when I go to the seaside with my family, I'm very worried about the grass,' Andrea Sanminiatelli explains. 'It is very difficult to maintain a lawn in central Italy, because of the Mediterranean climate. It is hot and dry, unlike the English climate. When it rains, I can relax a little bit. The garden is hard work all year round and the upkeep is also very expensive. It is the visitors who get the most pleasure from the garden, not the owner.'

The family first opened the estate to visitors in 1990, and it is necessary to come up with new ideas all the time in order to keep the project going. The ancient church is a popular choice for weddings, and receptions are often held in the garden. Since a couple of years ago, horticultural courses have been held in the newly restored glasshouse, along with botany courses for the blind. And there are many plans for the future. Russell Page left a lot of notes behind, and the Sanminiatellis are gradually trying to realize his plans and fulfil his wishes. The next project may be a lake for aquatic plants in the woods – dedicated to the two daughters.

'I love this place,' says Andrea Sanminiatelli. 'Whenever I go away, I always feel like there is something very special about coming home. I see it as my duty to maintain San Liberato for the benefit of future generations.'

A RIOT OF ROSES
CREATED BY UMBERTA PATRIZI 1980S

Palazzo Patrizi

Giuliano

The garden of Palazzo Patrizi is a riot of roses of all varieties, growing freely as bushes or climbing decoratively over the walls.

It is the Feast of the Roses and market day in the village of Giuliano. Marchioness Umberta Patrizi stands outside the entrance to the palace, speaking to a neighbour. The historical name of the castle is Castello Giuliano and over the centuries many important families have lived here, but the Patrizis, a papal family who were patrons of Caravaggio, have owned the estate since 1546.

In the dramatic rocky landscape north of Rome, Umberta Patrizi, a passionate rose-grower, has created an abundantly flowering garden, with the main focus – of course – on roses. Once a year, in May, there is a Feast of the Roses in the small village. It attracts people from the whole area who come to visit the market in the piazza outside the castle gates and to get a guided tour of the garden.

Castello Giuliano was originally a fortress built for defence. The area has been inhabited for thousands of years. There are still traces of the Etruscan people who lived here before and during Roman times. The area is below the volcanic Tolfa mountain, and archaeological finds have been made of Etruscan artistic graves which were dug out of the porous tufa rocks. The village of Giuliano is not far from the country estate of San Liberato by Lake Bracciano (see page 60), and the growing conditions are just as good here, except when the roots of the roses reach pockets of air and gas in the porous volcanic soil.

The Marchioness, who is the sole gardener, is wearing a pair of sturdy boots, and you get the feeling that this is a person who is not afraid of hard work. The garden

Red and pink roses climb the stairs of the castle.

is informal and can be described as a landscape garden with plantings following the slopes and sheer drops in the landscape. The solid, smooth stone walls of the castle are covered by red climbing roses. The walk continues and a long avenue of the snowy-white *Rosa* 'Iceberg' leads to the back of a charming large garden pavilion. On the way there, you pass a magnolia relative: the tulip tree (*Liriodendron tulipifera*), whose flowers are lime green and creamy white.

The castle is surrounded by lush bushes, foxgloves, myrtle and light blue and electric blue ceanothus. The borders contain roses, and tall thriving perennials of varieties which are common in English gardens but rare in the dry and hot climate of the Mediterranean. The colours of the flowers are striking in the afternoon light. A performance is taking place on the lawn in front of the border. A girl is dancing across the grass and the white material of her dress rustles around the elegant roses, peonies and foxgloves.

A grand stone pine stands in the middle of the large lawn, spreading its branches like an umbrella protecting the grass below. It's rare to find healthy, lush lawns in Italy, where a lot of watering and maintenance is necessary to keep them green in the soaring heat.

The densely planted garden area is surrounded by a path, below which is the forest where roe deer are hunted, says Umberta's daughter Luce, who shows me around. After a while we reach a cave covered in ferns, lichens and mosses. It is one of the many Etruscan graves in the area. In other parts of the garden, remnants of an old Roman wall can be seen.

Umberta Patrizi has bred new rose varieties which she has named after her five children. Luce shows me the rose named in her honour: Lucetta. The other roses are Marie-Louise, Graham, Thomas and Emanuel. When the sun sets in the west, the garden is enveloped in a warm orange glow. Even the roses take on a new colour in the evening sun.

The foxglove (*Digitalis purpurea*), with large rosettes of leaves and pretty bell-shaped flowers strung along a tall stalk, is abundant in all of Umberta's plantings.

A BOTANICAL GARDEN ON THE HILLS OF ROME
DESIGNED BY PIETRO PIROTTA 1883

Orto Botanico

Trastevere, Rome

Opposite
Top left Rome seen through cherry trees, in the Japanese Garden.
Top right In the shade below a hickory tree, ferns unfold their fronds.
Bottom right The Palm Walk, with the European fan palm (*Chamaerops humilis*) in front of the taller California fan palm (*Washingtonia filifera*) and Canary Island date palm (*Phoenix canariensis*). The Fountain of the Tritons, designed by the architect Ferdinando Fuga in 1750, can be glimpsed in the background.
Bottom left A shocking-pink azalea flowers amidst lush green vegetation from Asia and Eastern Europe.

The botanical garden in Rome provides a 'green lung' for the city. Now State-owned and maintained by Università La Sapienza, it is situated in Trastevere, near Porta Settimiana, the River Tiber and Palazzo Corsino. From the entrance at Largo Cristina di Svezia, a straight path leads to the Fountain of the Tritons. The fountain is surrounded by palm trees, of which the smallest – the European fan palm (*Chamaerops humilis*) – has a stem that creeps along the ground. Further back are taller palm trees, which combine with the smaller ones to create an effective play of lines behind the fountain.

Many visitors come to rest and relax in the shade of the elegant palms: Canary Island date palm (*Phoenix canariensis*), California fan palm (*Washingtonia filifera*) and Jelly palm (*Butia*). Others are more interested in the plants and choose a path towards the Gianicolo slope where the Rose Garden can be found. It contains a selection of the ornamental roses which were common in the Baroque gardens of Rome during the seventeenth and eighteenth centuries. Further up is a tall hickory tree (*Carya illinoinensis*) which shades the ferns. The bamboo copse to the left before the turning is worth a closer inspection. A narrow path leads in among the many varieties, and suddenly it's like being in the middle of a Chinese bamboo wood. It's funny how plants can affect the atmosphere. The Japanese Garden at the top of the park is relatively new and the cherries are full of beautiful pink blooms. The gardeners have created elegant still lifes of Oriental plants. A courting couple are sitting in the grass below a spring-flowering tree, taking in the panoramic view of the city below. On my way back, I pass a Baroque monument – a water staircase which is gradually becoming part of nature. It is overgrown by mosses and lichens, and in consequence looks far more interesting than if it were cleaned. The glasshouses at the bottom of the park contain orchids, succulents and tropical plants, but also a laboratory for botanists.

BAROQUE GARDEN
DESIGNED FOR PIETRO ALDOBRANDINI
BY GIACOMO DELLA PORTA AND CARLO MADERNO FROM 1598
WATERWORKS BY ORAZIO OLIVIERI

Villa Aldobrandini

Frascati

Near the piazza in Frascati outside Rome is the towering Villa Aldobrandini. The garden was designed by Giacomo della Porta (and completed by Carlo Maderno) for Pietro Aldobrandini, nephew of Pope Clement VIII. The design was inspired by contemporary gardens at Villa Lante, Villa D'Este (see pages 20, 34) and Villa Medici in Pratolino, and Giovanni Guerra was commissioned to make drawings of those gardens so that the designers of Villa Aldobrandini knew what they had to surpass.

In front of the villa there are three imposing terraces, but the most spectacular effects are to be found at the back, where a semicircular retaining wall cut into the hillside forms a water theatre. From his upstairs bedroom window Pietro had a view across a water staircase and twin columns. He could watch the water cascade down the steep hill, then come to a sudden halt as it was forced up inside the columns. From the top of the columns the water would spiral down in elegant swirls, to reach a final crescendo at a globe held by a majestic statue of Atlas.

The water theatre behind the Villa Aldobrandini, its centrepiece the statue of Atlas, with the magnificent water staircase and twin columns towering above.

LEVANDAM · OPPORTVNO SECESSV

CAMPANIA

A GARDEN IN A VOLCANIC LANDSCAPE

DESIGNED BY RUSSELL PAGE IN COLLABORATION WITH SUSANA WALTON FROM 1956

La Mortella

Ischia

Pages 72–3 Along the dramatic coastline between Sorrento and Salerno, seaside villages like Positano and Amalfi cling to the steep mountainsides.

Above Susana Walton's favourite plant is *Victoria amazonica*, the world's largest water lily.

Opposite The house is at the foot of Mount Zaro. The egg-shaped pool below contains three lava stones; the Egyptian blue water lily (*Nymphaea caerulea*) floats on the water, and the banks have been planted with *Gunnera manicata* and the blue fan palm (*Brahea armata*).

A piece of land in a ravine with a hard crust of lava and breathtaking views across the Bay of Naples; this is what the composer Sir William Walton and his Argentinian wife, Susana, fell in love with one day fifty years ago. Today, the rock-hard ground has been transformed into a thriving garden full of exotic plants from across the world.

'The fact is,' Lady Walton explains, 'that all the income from William's music, royalties and concerts was invested in the garden.'

There is not a person in sight when the beautiful copper gate opens automatically. The location is on a small suburban street just north of the town of Forio on the island of Ischia. This is where southern Italy's most ambitious private garden can be found. Immediately inside the entrance stands a 450-year-old olive tree. Regarded as holy in Antiquity, the olive tree represents peace and tranquillity, and is a fitting symbol for Sir William and Lady Walton, who sought at La Mortella a quiet place for their creative work, far away from the pressures of London life.

The atmosphere is magical and intense. It is very humid, and beautiful evening light dapples through the lush, green vegetation. The ground is covered in ferns. A small plaque describes a tree with fan-shaped leaves: it is the ancient maidenhair tree (*Ginkgo biloba*) – a 200-million-year-old relic, bearing the same genes today. The ginkgo is at its most beautiful in late autumn when the green leaves turn bright yellow.

Lady Walton is waiting at the villa, which is carved into the rock face. With a clear voice and a firm handshake she welcomes us to La Mortella – the place of myrtles.

The geology of La Mortella, at the foot of the hill of Zaro, is the consequence of a violent earthquake some ten or twenty thousand years ago, which filled the ravine with lava. When the Waltons were about to purchase the property in the mid-1950s, many of their friends tried to talk them out of it. But their minds were made up; they were

Opposite Contained in a canal inspired by Moorish garden art, a stream of water catches the light as it scissors downwards and finally comes to rest in a beautifully carved basin.

enthralled by the rocks. The lava which had solidified in the ravine had to be hacked away piece by piece. There were no machines or electricity on the island of Ischia in the 1950s, so it all had to be done by sheer muscle power. It was painfully slow work, but the reward was the abundance of fertile soil underneath the hard lava crust.

When the ravine was finally excavated, the building of the terraces could begin; this took another seven years. To design their garden, the Waltons hired Russell Page. He was inspired by the rocky terrain and wanted nature itself to form the layout, so he suggested a garden design in the shape of a rough 'L', with the main axis turning sharply to the left at 90 degrees.

'Russell Page told me that he had never worked as hard as those first three days in 1956 when the basic layout was planned,' Lady Walton says. 'I followed him everywhere and wrote down every single word he said. His instructions kept me busy for more than a decade.'

Page had two main pieces of advice: 'Don't plant one, plant a hundred,' and 'Keep the large rocks free of vegetation, so that the dramatic character isn't lost.' A third consideration was the client – because Sir William was a composer, the theme for the garden was to be harmony, silence and tranquillity.

The island of Ischia is famous for its warm water springs, but in the 1950s there was no communal water supply. For the initial planting, the Waltons had to arrange for water to be delivered by lorry loads. In addition, a cistern was built at the top of the mountain for the collection of rainwater. The planting was based on palm trees and tough succulents that would survive in the dry conditions. Page suggested a mixture of tree ferns, yuccas, aloes and agaves, plants with distinct and different foliage that would create a strong architectural expression. Straw mats were hung across the valley to protect the young plants from the burning sunshine, and give them a chance to gain a foothold.

Today, a thick band of the silvery-blue fan palm (*Brahea armata*), originally from Mexico, grows in front of the house. The palms flower to great effect, with catkins 3 metres (10 feet) long reaching down to the ground. One of Russell Page's favourite plants, blue chalk sticks (*Senecio serpens*) from South Africa, provides ground cover.

Lady Walton has a passion for tree ferns, or cycads. They can be traced back to Jurassic times, 200 million years ago, when dinosaurs roamed the earth. The cycads, which can subsist on carbon dioxide alone, were the only plants to survive an era when volcanoes were active. Today the cycads huddle together in a lush thicket, almost like a miniature rainforest. The tree ferns are kept moist thanks to a clever irrigation system with spouts attached to the trees. Lady Walton has positioned orchids and other plants on the trunks to enhance the exotic tropical effect.

We follow the steps up through the cycads to the glasshouse which is dedicated to one particular plant, *Victoria amazonica*. This, the world's largest water lily, originating from the Amazon swamps, is Lady Walton's most loved botanical project. The giant pie-dish-shaped leaves can reach a diameter of 2.5 metres (8 feet), and the spiky leaves are said to be so strong that South American fishermen can use them as stepping stones when crossing water.

In 1966, Russell Page returned to the island to modify the design of the garden at La Mortella. The house had now been constructed; the Waltons had followed Page's advice and built it to the south, carved into the steep hillside with space for the garden in front. Russell compared the house to a Moorish palace and wanted the garden to reflect the garden traditions of Islam, with enclosed spaces, fountains and water channels. The island now had a communal water supply and so it was possible to construct a trio of fountains running in a straight line, starting by one of the lava rocks in front of the house.

A large egg-shaped pool with a tall water spout was created as the focal point of the garden. Here the beautiful sacred lotus (*Nelumbo nucifera*) grows. She unfolds her petals early in the morning; a raindrop has settled in the middle of a leaf and is dancing around without being absorbed. Near by is the rhubarb-like *Gunnera manicata*.

Falling softly down from the spout, the water continues invisibly underground to the second fountain, adorned with a lotus bud. The stream of water continues along the main axis. This part of the garden makes reference to the Lion Court in the gardens of the Alhambra in Granada, where two channels form a cross of flowing water, inspired by the Persian water channels found in oases.

The last fountain was built in 1983, in the shape of an octagon. It was Page's gift to Sir William Walton on his eightieth birthday. Sadly, both Russell Page and Sir William died before the fountain was finished, but, says Lady Walton, 'William was absolutely thrilled to finally have a flowing, glittering band of water as a backdrop in the valley. He could really enjoy it just by thinking of what it would look like – the water bubbling up from the terracotta lotus bud.'

On our way up to the mountain, we pass the orchid house with hummingbirds from all over the world. Lady Walton comes here every morning to feed the birds and listen to their song. The clever private mountain lift can just about take two people to the summit. Lady Walton has transformed the previously totally overgrown area into a mystical and diverse garden plateau with a slightly Oriental feel.

A Thai tea house, which she brought back from Bangkok, sits far away amidst the greenery. The best time for quiet contemplation in the house is early morning, when the lotus flower unfolds its pink petals. Along the meandering stream, we pass the tall *Canna striata,* with fiery red flowers and stripy leaves, and a larger copse with the distinctive red stems of a *Nandina domestica*, which resembles bamboo but actually belongs to the *Berberis* family. The slow-flowing water is flanked by Japanese maples and banana trees.

Lady Walton has created a memorial to her husband on the mountain. There is a pyramid-shaped lava rock here, which William claimed as 'his rock' on the very day they decided to buy the property. This is by far the most beautiful part of the garden, with spectacular views of the sea, Vesuvius and the sun setting in the west.

Opposite, clockwise from top left The flower of *Tillandsia dyeriana*; *Caladium* 'White Christmas'; the seed pod and pinky-white petals of the sacred lotus (*Nelumbo nucifera*).

A TROPICAL GARDEN ON ROMAN FOUNDATIONS

CREATED BY BARON LABONIA, WILLIAM WALDORF ASTOR AND MARIANO AND RITA PANE FROM 1868

Above The nymphaeum is the oldest historical relic in the garden. Above the sarcophagus a stone lion ornaments a Roman wall.

Opposite A long pergola of chestnut poles leads to one of many archaeological finds that are placed about the garden, amidst the vegetation.

Villa Il Tritone

Sorrento

In AD 79 a giant tsunami, an after-effect of the volcanic eruption of Mount Vesuvius which destroyed the cities of Pompeii and Herculaneum, came crashing into the Bay of Naples and drowned the promontory where Villa Il Tritone is situated today.

There was already a villa at Il Tritone two thousand years ago. If you lean out over the balustrade, you can glimpse the remains of Roman foundations just above the surface of the turquoise water. The villa is said to have belonged to Agrippa Posthumus (12 BC–AD 14), grandson of the Roman Emperor Augustus and son of Marcus Vipsanius Agrippa who built the original Pantheon in Rome. Agrippa decorated his house in Sorrento with rare marble and Egyptian art, including yellow marble columns which were already a thousand years old. The collection is still there, rediscovered in the ash at the bottom of the sea and recovered during the nineteenth and twentieth centuries. Antique objects are an integral part of the garden, covered by tropical plants.

The promontory was rediscovered after a thousand years, in the thirteenth century, and a convent for the nuns of St Clare was built on the foundations of the Roman villa. In the nineteenth century the estate passed into private hands, when it was bought by antique dealer Baron Labonia of Calabria. He built the house and started to plan the garden, inserting archaeological pieces. In 1905 Villa Il Tritone was bought by William Waldorf Astor, who was then American Ambassador in Rome. Like so many others, Astor fell in love with Sorrento. He enlarged the property by buying neighbouring land, introduced the exotic plants and had walks designed following the English style. Mariano and Rita Pane from Rome bought Villa Il Tritone in 1973.

On the steep cliff edge is a wall that separates the garden from the sea. It was built by Astor to protect the plants from the fierce winds, and to provide a calmer, more private atmosphere. My initial disappointment at the partially obscured view turns

Above A walk bordered by oleanders, with sheltering palm trees behind.

Opposite The balustrade bordering the lake was built by William Astor. Il Tritone, the bearded sea god, and the other carved heads are the work of the artist Sir Lawrence Alma-Tadema.

into fascination when I start to catch glimpses through the openings in the wall. Through one of the windows I can just make out Mount Vesuvius, through another I see the Bay of Naples. Far away is the outline of the island of Capri. In May and August, the different views are further embellished by racemes of wisteria and floribunda that drape over the wall.

Villa Il Tritone's tropical vegetation is magical. A stroll through the garden feels like being in a hothouse. Long straight paths overhung with lush greenery and flanked by large exotic trees create interesting vistas along corridors of climbers. Each sightline ends at an antique statue or a sarcophagus, an antique capital or a window in the wall with a sea view. There is a pergola made of chestnut poles, with sunlight dappling down through the fragile branches. The Panes' dog is asleep on the path in the middle of a group of palm trees. Both Mariano and Rita take great interest in the garden, as do their three children who are now grown up and have left home.

'Gardening is the most noble occupation in the world,' says Mariano. 'If you plant a seed and give it all your attention, you can be sure of getting something in return. If you raise children, you never know what might happen.'

Rita adds: 'The plant responds to what you do, you give love and the plant responds with the same intensity. With people it is not the same, anything can happen, nothing is predictable.'

Rita, who takes the main responsibility for the garden, exercises restraint in the number of plants she grows in any one section, preferring to let one type of plant spread out over a large area. This gives a refined and harmonious overall feeling. The emphasis is on shapes of leaves and shades of green rather than on bright colour. One part of the garden is dominated by the African lily (*Agapanthus*). When it is in bloom in July, the blue spherical flowers float in the air like decorative balls. The leaves are shiny, spear-like and springy, and provide interest all year round. Many of the palm trees come from Brazil and have striking trunks of an almost steely grey.

It is an exotic garden. A group of healthy cactuses seem very much at home; in the distance I spot some thriving banana trees. The tropical plants have acclimatized and seem to be thriving: palms, cycads, cypresses, orange trees, eucalyptuses, pines and jacarandas. There are many varieties with fascinating names: the bottle tree (*Brachychiton*) from Mexico, the coral tree (*Erythrina crista-galli*) from Brazil, white bird of paradise (*Strelitzia nicolai*) from South America, *Jacaranda* from Chile, the sago palm

(*Cycas revoluta*) from Polynesia and Australia and the elegant European fan palm (*Chamaerops humilis*).

Rita loves waking up to the sound of birdsong, which is no longer very common in Italy. She explains that she feels very privileged: 'Once we found a very unusual flower which we hadn't planted. It belongs to a rare family and parts of it are like black velvet. We think a bird on its way north from Africa may have carried the seed in its beak. When it touched down here, the seed found the right microclimate to germinate. The flower is still growing here in our garden.'

On the ferry to Capri, I turn around and look back towards Villa Il Tritone, built into the cliff at the tip of the promontory. The afternoon sun is glittering in the water. It's easy to understand why Agrippa Posthumus, who could have settled anywhere he wanted in the Roman Empire, chose to build his house on this particular spot.

AN ITALIAN VERSAILLES

BAROQUE GARDEN DESIGNED BY LUIGI AND CARLO VANVITELLI FOR CHARLES III OF BOURBON FROM 1752

ENGLISH LANDSCAPE GARDEN DESIGNED BY JOHN ANDREW GRAEFER FOR MARIA CAROLINA OF AUSTRIA FROM 1815

Palazzo Reale

Caserta

The closest you could find in Italy to Louis XIV's grand garden of Versailles is La Reggia di Caserta. In the 1740s Charles III of Bourbon, ruler of the Kingdom of Naples and the Two Sicilies, under the threat of attack by the British fleet, determined to move his capital away from the sea. He had a royal palace with a Baroque garden built some twenty-two miles inland from Naples, at the foot of the Tifatini mountains. The establishment at Caserta, an estate of 300 acres, illustrates the immense power of the kingdom of Naples and its Bourbon rulers. The King commissioned the Dutch-born architect Luigi Vanvitelli to design a palace and a park that could compete with Versailles. And Vanvitelli took him at his word.

The central perspective is spectacular. Like a gradually sloping mountain river, the axis 'flows' between the entrance to the palace and the cascades, a distance of two miles past groups of statues, ponds and long, narrow lawns. The middle axis is flanked by a dense, perfectly clipped curtain of two rows of oaks and camphor trees. On special occasions, the ponds and the trees are illuminated at night-time. Everything is on a grand scale. To the left is a stylish avenue, with tall treetops meeting in a transparent arch, shimmering in light green. If you continue through the avenue towards the eastern corner of the park, you will reach the large lake. It is 270 metres (885 feet) long and was once used for entertainments including simulated naval battles. The water for the fountains and ponds in the park was supplied via the Caroline aqueduct, which took sixteen years to build. Luigi Vanvitelli was responsible for the construction, which rose to 60 metres (200 feet) above ground. When he died in 1773, his son Carlo continued the work in the park.

The two-mile-long avenue leading in a straight line across the park to the palace is punctuated by fountains with mythological themes.

Above left Sunlight dapples down through the foliage along an avenue.

Above right The central axis of the garden leads to the cascade and the enormous water staircase. Below is the magnificent Fountain of Diana and Actaeon.

Many of the fountains along the central axis have themes inspired by Classical mythology or by Ovid's *Metamorphoses*. In the richly decorated Fountain of the Dolphins, the different levels create twelve miniature waterfalls, and the same number of lakes. As in the water staircase at Villa Lante (see page 20), the bottom has deliberately been given an uneven surface in order to bring life to the water, which seems to be dancing on its way downwards.The Fountain of Aeolus (the wind god) is 3 metres (10 feet) deep and it holds an astonishing amount of water – hundreds of thousands of cubic metres. There are cavities behind the waterfall which can be entered. Towards the end of the long basin is the Fountain of Ceres, where dolphins mingle with the sea gods of mythology, the Tritons. They send water jets high into the air, surrounded by the statues of the rivers Simeto and Oreto, nymphs and the goddess Ceres. Beyond the small waterfalls is the Fountain of Venus and Adonis. A kneeling Venus takes the hand of Adonis and asks him to take care during the hunt. But danger is lurking in the shape of a jealous god, Mars, who has taken on the appearance of a wild boar and is about to kill Adonis. I leave them to their tragic fate and reach the impressive Fountain of Diana and Actaeon. Diana, the goddess of hunting, and also the patron of chastity, is on the right and on the left is Actaeon defending himself against dogs which are tearing him apart.

The Bath of Venus, set among ruins in a shady glade.

At the end of the long central axis a small gate leads to a wonderful English landscape garden, created in the early nineteenth century by John Andrew Graefer for Maria Carolina of Austria, wife of Ferdinand IV. The transition from the formal garden to this open park with tall elegant trees on wide open lawns is refreshing.

At the Queen's behest Graefer designed and created; he constructed hills and valleys, temples, nymphaea and artificial ruins. Since the Queen was very interested in unusual plants, exotic trees were brought from the newly discovered parts of the world. The garden was once known as 'The Botanical Garden of the Royal House'. During my stroll along the snaking footpaths, I pass one beautiful tree after another: a cedar of Lebanon, cypresses, pine trees, magnolias and cactuses. One of my aims is to see the Bath of Venus. I find her in a glade, amongst ruins and shady trees. She is crouching on a moss-covered stone, surrounded by magical, lush greenery. The setting and atmosphere are like a beautiful work of art.

On my way back along the water axis, I stop and turn around. Far away I can see the water cascading down the slope. It reminds me of the water staircases in the gardens of Villa Lante and Villa Farnese (see page 54) – except in terms of size: this cascade is huge. The park at Palazzo Reale is the last grand garden of its kind laid out in Italy. From the end of the eighteenth century, garden style was mainly dominated by France and England.

TERRACE WITH VIEWS OF THE AMALFI COAST

DESIGNED BY NICOLA MANSI FOR ERNEST WILLIAM BECKETT 1910–15

Above The cloister garden with its twisted columns and pointed Gothic arches dates from the fourteenth century.

Opposite Dilapidated statues of Roman origin guard the edge of the garden. The Terrazzo dell'Infinito (Terrace of Infinity) offers breathtaking views of the Amalfi coast and the Bay of Salerno.

Villa Cimbrone

Ravello

The road along the coast to the south of Naples must be one of the most scenic routes in Europe. Every turn of the steering wheel gives you a new view of the beautiful landscape and the dark blue sea. Having passed the dramatically situated town of Positano we find the sign for Ravello, just before Amalfi. All along the four miles of steep uphill road other cars seem rather too close for comfort. It feels a little hazardous.

People in the town of Ravello are used to tourists and we are pleased to discover that they have provided parking spaces. The attraction is the two villas, Cimbrone and Rufolo, of which the first is reached via a narrow pedestrian road. When art dealer Ernest William Beckett, later Lord Grimthorpe, bought the estate in the early 1900s, he commissioned architect Nicola Mansi from Ravello to create a garden. The overgrown edge of the cliff was transformed into a romantic park. Nicola Mansi began with a long, wide walk, a central line starting from the entrance to the villa and ending at the long terrace. He created different environments within the park: pergolas, small temples and airy wrought-iron domed gazebos.

Lord Grimthorpe is said to have received advice from Vita Sackville-West, creator of the famous garden at Sissinghurst Castle in England. Vita and her husband, Harold Nicolson, were among the many regular guests at the villa. However, there are few similarities between Villa Cimbrone and Sissinghurst: the two gardens are situated in very different climates, and come from different traditions.

To the left of the entrance is a well-preserved medieval gem: a monastery, probably dating from the fourteenth century, with a charming small courtyard in Arab-Sicilian-Norman style containing a well and groups of pots. This courtyard is surrounded by a covered loggia, supported by twisted columns and Gothic pointed arches, and leads

Opposite
Top left A narrow path, bordered by a curved balustrade with elegantly shaped urns, leads from the town to the garden of Villa Cimbrone.
Top right Tall umbrella pines shade the garden room known as the Tea Room, where annuals are planted in bright-coloured patterns.
Bottom right At the end of a wooden wisteria-covered pergola is a bronze statue of the young David, with the head of Goliath at his feet.
Bottom left The Temple of Bacchus, the tomb of Lord Grimthorpe, who died in London in 1917. On the frieze of the temple appear the words of Catullus (*Poem 31*, lines 7–10):

O quid solutis est beatius curis,
cum mens onus reponit, ac peregrino
labore fessi venimus larem ad nostrum,
desideratoque acquiescimus lecto?

What is more blessed than when the mind,
Cares dispelled, puts down its burden,
And we return, tired from travelling, to our home
To rest on the bed we have longed for?

to an open crypt which was used as a burial place for nuns and monks but is today an outdoor dining room – in the tradition of the ancient Roman *triclinium* – for guests at the villa, now a hotel. From the tables, there is a stunning view of the sea through the silhouettes of columns. In the foreground, elegant hydrangeas are displaying a range of pink shades.

On my way to the tempting terrace at the edge of the cliff, I walk past the Tea Room, which is an open area decorated with remains of Antiquity: statues, enormous urns and an exquisite bronze sculpture of a slender roe deer. Near by is the rose garden, with geometrical flower beds. The road continues towards something resembling a Roman bridge, covered with flowering blue and white wisterias. To the left is an immaculate green lawn surrounded by tall hedges. It is easy to imagine guests playing boules or croquet here. Or perhaps it was in this calm, sheltered area that the great actress Greta Garbo used to sit and read. A plaque with her name and that of her lover, the conductor Leopold Stokowski, can be seen on the façade as a reminder of their visit to Villa Cimbrone in 1938.

I turn right, down towards the Mound of Mercury. Mercury was not only the Roman messenger god, but also patron of the merchants of ancient Rome. The Greek equivalent was Hermes, and he can be seen at the edge of the cliff. *Hermes at Rest* is a copy of a bronze statue of the Lisippo school that can be seen at the Museo Archeologico Nazionale in Naples. The view from the Temple of Bacchus next to Hermes gives you an unusual perspective on the landscape. The roads meander through the many vineyards and create a miniature world along the Amalfi coastline.

A wide walk, the Path of Eternity, leads to the Terrace of Infinity, where the sea meets the sky. Despite the rain-laden skies, it gives a refreshing feeling of freedom to stand here, surrounded by the marble busts of Roman rulers, and gaze out across the deep blue sea.

LABORE FESSI VENIMUS LAREM

SETTING FOR
A WAGNER OPERA
RESTORED BY FRANCIS NEVILLE REID 1880S

Villa Rufolo

Ravello

Above The view from the terrace, over the Bay of Salerno.

Opposite Boston ivy (*Parthenocissus tricuspidata*) has grown over the façade of the palace.

Villa Rufolo was originally built in the 1270s for the Rufolo family. During the Middle Ages, the tall Torre Maggiore was used as a lookout for pirates and corsairs who plagued the Amalfi coast. The palace is built around a courtyard with surrounding loggias richly decorated in Moorish style. In front of the palace, to the south, is an unusual garden loggia that is rather similar to the crypt at the Villa Cimbrone, with cross-vaulting and slender columns grouped to form arcades which open out into the garden. It was once used as a cool outdoor dining area. The garden on the upper terraces contains cypresses and exotic plants such as cycads, yuccas and palms, as well as brightly coloured annuals planted in formal borders. When the Rufolo family sold the palace in 1588, both the house and the garden were left to decay. It was not until the mid-1800s that it was restored by a new owner, the Scottish botanist Francis Neville Reid. Just as at the Villa Cimbrone, the terraces open out unexpectedly to captivating views of earth, sea and sky. When Wagner brought his family here in the 1880s he said that he felt he had discovered the setting of Klingsor's magic garden in the second act of *Parsifal*. The Ravello Classical Music Festival is held here every summer, with the Bay of Salerno as a backdrop.

A GARDEN FOR THE SOUL

CREATED BY AXEL MUNTHE 1900S

Above An Egyptian sphinx gazes out towards the sea, the Sorrento peninsula and Mount Vesuvius.

Opposite A white-pillared pergola covered in wisteria and jasmine marks the boundary of the garden.

Villa San Michele

Capri

The garden and sculpture gallery of the Villa San Michele lie just beyond the piazza of Anacapri, the highest village on the steep cliff of the island of Capri. From here magnificent views open up across the Bay of Naples to Mount Vesuvius and the coastline south of Sorrento. In spring when the broom is in flower the mountain slope is a striking golden yellow. San Michele was created by the Swedish physician and writer Axel Munthe, who believed that the views were the most important aspects of a garden – 'the soul needs space'.

An Imperial summer villa once stood on this spot, and today three thousand items from Classical times are displayed in Villa San Michele and the garden. Many of the antiquities in the garden came from the early villa; others were gifts which Axel Munthe received from grateful patients. Among the treasures is a marble head of Ulysses, a Roman copy of the Greek original of the fifth century BC. There is also a bronze copy of *Hermes at Rest* (the original is in the Museo Archeologico Nazionale di Napoli and another copy is at Villa Cimbrone, see page 90). A wonderful long white-pillared pergola covered in blue *Wisteria sinensis* and white *Jasminum nudiflorum* winds round the edge of the garden. Among the greenery are pots that are filled with bulbs (tulips or hyacinths) or annuals, depending on the season. By the covered loggia at the end, an Egyptian granite sphinx gazes out towards the point where sky and sea become one.

In the early morning, light dapples down through the foliage and illuminates peonies, hydrangeas, camellias, pomegranates, wild orange trees, bananas, palm trees and vines on the slope up towards the ruined Barabossa castle. After several unsuccessful attempts to grow the nordic birch tree (*Betula*), the gardeners were advised to keep the young plants in a refrigerator during their first winters. They did this for three years in succession. One of the plants survived and every year on 19 March it opens its tender, light green leaves.

THERMAL BATHS IN AN EXOTIC GARDEN
Exotic Garden Created by Luigi Silvestro Camerini from 1947
Water Garden Designed by Ermanno Casasco for Paolo Fulceri Camerini from 1988

Negombo
Ischia

Negombo occupies a sheltered spot between Mount Zaro and Mount Vico, on the shores of the Bay of San Montano in the north-west corner of the volcanic island of Ischia. When the botanist Duke Luigi Silvestro Camerini first came here in 1947 he immediately fell in love with the place. He bought all the land in the bay and arranged for exotic trees and plants which he had come across on his travels around the world to be shipped over, so that he could create a botanical garden. He also mapped the natural hot springs.

During the 1970s and 1980s the garden was open to visitors, offering thermal baths in the surroundings of the botanical gardens. Then in 1988 Luigi Camerini's son, Paolo Fulceri Camerini, employed landscape architect Ermanno Casasco to give the park a form and a structure. This he has done in a very poetic and talented way, creating thermal baths of every type and carefully integrating them among the tropical plants introduced by Luigi and the natural vegetation of holm-oaks, laurels, maritime pines, olive trees and carobs.

It is amazing to think of the hot water of the springs rushing under one's feet and then cascading out of the mountain as a waterfall, or being calmly collected in pools of every imaginable shape. The garden has 67 volcanic steam springs, 29 catch basins and 103 hot springs.

It is not simply relaxing to spend a day in Negombo; it is also very much an aesthetic experience. Who would not want to sit in a pool of water at a temperature of 30–40°C (85–105°F), surrounded by beautiful rocks and lush greenery and a fantastic sea view? It is a glimpse of paradise. The Greeks who settled here in the bay in 770 BC might well have agreed.

Opposite One of the thermal pools, surrounded by lush greenery.

ORANGE TREES AND MAJOLICA TILES
DESIGNED BY
ANTONIO DOMENICO VACCARO 1742

Cloister Garden of Santa Chiara

Naples

The Santa Chiara Cloister Garden lies in the most ancient part of Naples, near the long Spaccanapoli street which divides the eastern and western parts of the city. The area was once the centre of the forum of the Graeco-Roman city. The church of Santa Chiara dates back to the fourteenth century and is part of a working monastery. The garden as we see it today was laid out by Antonio Domenico Vaccaro in 1742. Vaccaro created an environment of pergolas, balustrades and pillars, most of them decorated with brilliantly coloured majolica tiles with motifs of landscapes, triumphal processions and scenes from mythology. A more traditional but equally interesting cloister garden is to be found near by at San Gregorio Armeno.

The orange trees in the cloister garden are almost overshadowed by the eighteenth-century columns and benches richly decorated with majolica tiles.

The Minerva Garden

Salerno

A GARDEN OF SIMPLES
CREATED BY MATTEO SILVATICO
LATE THIRTEENTH AND
EARLY FOURTEENTH CENTURIES

Squeezed in between the houses and the tiny streets of Salerno are the remains of the physic garden created during the late thirteenth and early fourteenth centuries by Matteo Silvatico, an expert on medicinal plants. According to the town of Salerno, the Minerva Garden was the first small botanical garden in Europe to grow simples, herbs used for therapeutic purposes. Terraces climbing steeply upwards make the most of the small space. The staircase leading up to the different levels is built on top of the ancient walls and supported by square pillars and lattice work with decorative climbing vines. From the top terrace there is a view of the historical part of the town, along with the harbour of Salerno and people going about their everyday life in the alleyways. Washing is hanging outside the windows and on balconies in the old town, and in the glittering water below I glimpse cargo ships in the harbour. The garden was restored with financial help from the European URBAN programme. Today there are few plants left, but the garden is well worth a visit for its historical value and its delightful atmosphere.

A long, steep staircase covered in vines bearing an abundance of grapes leads to the upper terrace.

TUSCANY

THE ARCHITECTS' FAVOURITE

ORIGINAL GARDEN CREATED BY ANDREA DI COSIMO LAPI
IN THE SEVENTEENTH CENTURY
WATER GARDEN CREATED BY GIOVANNA GHYKA AND MARTINO PORCINAI FROM 1900

Villa Gamberaia

Settignano

I am travelling from Lucca via Florence on my way to Settignano. After much criss-crossing and many complicated lane changes, the character of the surroundings begins to alter: city turns into countryside in just a few minutes. The road takes me upwards, and beautiful stone walls separate the road from the olive groves. The last challenge is a narrow city gate. With my wing mirrors folded in, I manage to steer my hired car into Via del Rossellino. The gate to Villa Gamberaia opens automatically and I have finally reached a garden that has been praised by architects and garden experts the world over.

What everyone admires about the Villa Gamberaia is its well-balanced proportions, which create a harmonious composition in a limited space. As the British landscape architect Cecil Pinsent writes in *Il Giardino Fiorito* (1931), 'after having walked in that garden, relatively small in size, one goes away with the impression of having spent more time there and having discovered more than was in reality the case.'

A dense avenue of cypresses leads up to the villa and there is a sense of calm. From the immaculate lawn, I can see the valley of the Arno and the Renaissance city of Florence. Tiny houses huddle together, and the famous silhouette of Brunelleschi's Duomo stands out like a big rust-coloured cake. Silent aeroplanes glide across the sky above the church spires. It's a great place to be – I feel as if I'm floating outside reality.

Pages 100–101 From the garden of La Foce, an avenue of cypresses can be seen zigzagging across the undulating landscape of Val d'Orcia.

Left The water parterre at Villa Gamberaia was created in the early twentieth century, replacing an eighteenth-century embroidered parterre. Its basic shape is that of a cloister garden with four rectangles divided by paths forming a cross with a circle in the middle. The curtain of clipped cypresses behind has eleven topiary 'windows' looking out on Florence. To the left is the long lawn that forms the centre axis of the garden.

Engraving by Giuseppe Zocchi showing the Villa Gamberaia, seen from Via del Rossellino, in 1744. It looks very much the same today. Note the low trees of the cypress walk at the entrance, and the small bridge which spans the road.

From the loggia on the first floor, the views across the Tuscan landscape are breathtaking. Far away is the Piazzale Michelangelo, and medieval turrets pierce the sky among the undulating hills as if in a fairy tale. I can almost see Dante riding out from Florence on his horse through the mist across the hills towards the paradise he describes in *The Divine Comedy*, which he wrote in the fourteenth century while in exile from his beloved home city of Florence.

The transformation from a simple summer house to a palatial villa began at the end of the sixteenth century, when terraces were laid out on the sloping hills. According to an inscription in the garden dated 1610, the house was in all probability founded by Zanobi Lapi. He built a grand villa: a typical Florentine house in a restrained style, a cube with elegant windows in the basement. The villa was later inherited by Andrea di Cosimo Lapi, who lived at La Gamberaia for fifty-nine years. It was he who laid out the seventeenth-century garden, which was adorned with grottoes, statues, vases, fountains and *giochi d'acqua* of every description. When he died, Villa Gamberaia passed into the ownership of Antonio and Piero Capponi.

In the early twentieth century, the then owner, the Serbian Princess Giovanna Ghyka, assisted by the talented gardener Martino Porcinai (father of landscape architect Pietro Porcinai – see page 128), transformed the parterre to the south of the villa into the water garden we see today. The layout of the garden follows the classical Renaissance design, with four rectangles split by four main walkways forming a cross with a small pond in the round space in the middle. But instead of patterns of planted beds the four main areas are water pools. The earlier parterre's low hedges of lavender and oleander have been replaced by box and yew in different shapes. These have been pruned creatively and rhythmically to different heights, and here and there the dark green hedges surround statues or urns containing lemon trees.

Behind the water parterre is an elegantly clipped hedge planted as an arcade around a pond. This beautiful cypress curtain has eleven topiary 'windows'. The tree next to it, *Phillyrea latifolia,* is cleverly pruned, its crown a perfect sphere trimmed twice a year by head gardener Silvano, who has worked at Villa Gamberaia for fifty years, and has had

Throughout the warm season, urns with citrus trees are placed inside the hedges of the water parterre. The hedges and the topiary cubes and hemispheres are all perfectly trimmed, as is the ball-shaped *Phillyrea latifolia*, at the far end near the cypress curtain.

the honour of pruning the tree for all that time. In order to reach the middle of the crown, he has ingeniously built a ladder inside the tree.

During the Renaissance and the Baroque periods, topiary – *ars topiaria*, 'garden art' – was considered to bring gardens to a higher intellectual level. It was felt that cutting shrubs into geometrical or natural shapes freed the garden from the 'chaos' of nature.

A short cut to the left behind the cypress arcade leads to a Corsican pine (*Pinus nigra* var. *Corsicana*). Behind this is a lush lawn 225 metres (750 feet) long, a perfect area for playing tennis, bowls or maybe croquet. Laid out by Andrea Capponi in the eighteenth century, the lawn is the centre of the garden and its main axis. It links the Arno Valley to a nymphaeum by the hillside. The transverse axis is roughly half as long – 105 metres (350 feet) – and leads from the villa's inner courtyard to the Grotto Garden. Alongside the lawn to the right is a beautifully decorated wall, hiding the Grotto Garden and a wooded area with centuries-old ilex trees (*Quercus ilex*). Periwinkle (*Vinca major*) and butcher's broom (*Ruscus aculeatus*) cover the ground. To the left are the main building and then some smaller houses, which used to be a chapel and an indoor tennis court, and have now been transformed into well-equipped guesthouses. To the right is a row of ten giant urns, which during April and May are filled with beautiful shocking-pink azaleas.

The Grotto Garden was built during the eighteenth century to link two levels – the wood and the Orangery. Here there are four female terracotta figures with faint smiles and flowers in their hair, representing the four seasons. In summer these are surrounded by flowering hydrangeas, roses and wisteria. As in other Renaissance gardens in the Rome area – for example, Villa d'Este and Villa Lante (see pages 34 and 20) – there are water jets which were originally meant to entertain guests. Unfortunately, here they no longer work. The sandstone balustrade is decorated with flowery motifs and the walls are covered in fossils and corals.

On the top terrace is the oldest house in the area, dating from the fifteenth century. This was the home of the Gamberelli family, famous for their stonework in the town of Pienza. From here, the olive groves in the valley are visible (olive oil is still produced at Villa Gamberaia today). In the beautiful Orangery next to the terrace, citrus plants

Opposite
Top There are lots of dogs, in the shape of beautiful sculptures, at Villa Gamberaia. They are the symbolic protectors of the property. In the background, the village of Settignano and the church of Santa Maria are visible, while Brunelleschi's dark-red Duomo can be glimpsed in the distance.
Below right A splendid bust of a woman on a richly decorated sandstone balustrade, in the Grotto Garden.
Below left The wonderful lawn is 225 metres (750 feet) long and forms a straight axis from the nymphaeum to the Corsican pine (*Pinus nigra* var. *Corsicana*), from where the view across the valley of the Arno is glorious. In April and May giant urns filled with shocking-pink azaleas are placed on the grass.

– lemon and orange trees, mandarins, grapefruits and kumquats – are kept in urns during winter. In warmer months, these urns are hidden inside the box hedges in the parterre or sun themselves in the courtyard outside the Orangery. A woman strolling past with an easel tells me that she teaches an art group from the United States who are using the Orangery as a studio for a month, staying in the guesthouses on the estate.

In December it is very cold in the estate office – 15°C outside, 5°C inside, which tells us something about the thickness of the walls. Thanks to two radiators and a cup of coffee I manage to keep warm. Luigi Zalum, the owner, enters wearing a cinnamon-coloured felt hat and a long sandy-beige coat.

His father-in-law, the industrialist Marcello Marchi, bought Villa Gamberaia after the Second World War. The Germans had used the house as their headquarters and kept maps, tables and war records there. When they retreated, a German officer ordered the villa to be burnt down, and an obedient soldier set fire to it with petrol, but fortunately did not entirely succeed. Bernard Berenson described La Gamberaia in his diary entry for 4 March 1948: 'Walked over to Villa Gamberaia, found it neglected, unkempt, grass not mown, trees with branches broken looking like elephants with broken tusks, the house burnt out with the beautiful courtyard fallen in, vases and stone animals on parapets thrown down and broken – and yet the place retains its charm, its power to inspire longing and dreams, sweet dreams.'

I ask Luigi Zalum to tell me the secret behind this very well-kept, beautifully proportioned garden. 'Water and fertilizer,' is his matter-of-fact answer. 'I also make sure I employ gardeners who know their job. I want the villa to be kept in a good condition for future generations, but the entrance fees aren't enough to cover everything.'

For three hundred years, the neighbours fought over the right to the three springs on the estate. Some years ago Luigi Zalum tired of the quarrelling and built a deep well. Another problem is the spring floods, which carry plants and soil from the mountains and threaten to damage the house. 'But despite all the worries, I'm emotionally attached to the estate – it's my destiny to keep the villa and to maintain it for the future,' says Zalum, before putting his wide-brimmed hat back on.

Leaving the garden I take a sharp turn with my Fiat and park in the village square. Caffe Schnuff is perfectly situated, with a view of the Santa Maria church and Piazza Tommaseo. I relax over a double espresso, and watch the people go about their business on the piazza.

ITALIAN-BRITISH GARDEN IN A LUNAR LANDSCAPE
CREATED BY IRIS ORIGO AND CECIL PINSENT 1926–39

The ancient wisteria on the pergola thrives despite the hot, dry and windy climate, and needs surprisingly little care. It has its origin in one mother plant which has spread over the long pergola, ending out in the hilly landscape.

La Foce

Val d'Orcia

Straight ahead of me, across the valley on the slope, I can see a zigzag-shaped avenue of cypresses. If I am not mistaken, I have seen the motif on a postcard in Siena. Is it a strange natural phenomenon or is it planted? The explanation can be found at the country estate of La Foce.

La Foce sits high on a mountain, to the south of Siena, at a junction between the towns of Pienza and Montepulciano, surrounded by soft undulating hills formed by the characteristic light yellow-brown chalky soil, *terra di Siena*. Here the British-American writer Iris Origo and her Italian husband Marquis Antonio Origo created a prosperous farm in the 1920s. They turned a former tavern and monastery dating back to 1498 into their private villa, and laid out a garden in the hilly terrain as a mixture of an Italian Renaissance garden and an English flower garden.

While waiting to be shown around the villa, I continue down the hill, past a beautifully aged storeroom door, to a viewing area. A very unusual landscape lies ahead of me. Barren but beautiful, it reminds me of pictures I've seen of the surface of the moon. The colour of the softly rounded hills changes with the seasons, and of course also depends on what crops are grown. Down in the valley, the River Orcia flows slowly before it joins an artificial lake, created in the 1920s. The volcanic Mount Amiata to the west is 1,400 metres (4,600 feet) high, and now has an extensive system of ski lifts.

Iris Origo was a famous author of several books, including her autobiography *Images and Shadows* (1970), in which she describes her upbringing in Tuscany. She was born in the early 1900s, the daughter of William Bayard Cutting Jnr, an American working in London, and his wife, Sybil. There was gardening in her background: at their home on Long Island in the United States, Westbrook, her paternal grandparents had a

The cypresses in the Lower Garden form the shape of a ship's bow. The trees are planted as a wall around the garden to provide protection from the biting wind that sweeps in from the north-west in the autumn.

collection of rare exotic trees from around the world which attracted visitors from all over the country.

Iris grew up with her mother at the famous Villa Medici in Fiesole. An only child in an academic environment, she enjoyed a rich social life with educational trips abroad. She married the Italian Antonio Origo and together they discovered La Foce, where they settled in 1926. *Foce* means opening or meeting place. The main building, an *osteria*, a cross between a hospital and a tavern, was probably designed by the Renaissance architect Baldassare Peruzzi. When the Origos arrived, there were fifteen small farms belonging to the estate. The ground was hard and dry and the area poor. Iris and Antonio were keen to develop the estate and help the farmers to provide for themselves; they also wanted to offer health care and education for the children. The construction of an artificial lake drained the valley and loosened the mud, making cultivation of the land possible.

The main axis of the garden is lined by box hedges, their immaculate lines broken by carefully clipped topiary hemispheres.

In her memoirs, Iris describes how she looked out across the deserted landscape and was struck by a longing for 'the gentle, trim Florentine landscape of my childhood or for green English fields and big trees – and most of all, for a pretty house and garden to come home to in the evening.' In 1927 she contacted a British friend, the architect Cecil Pinsent, who had worked on several projects around Florence: houses, interiors and gardens. Pinsent had a great ability to 'listen to the landscape' and to respect the natural movement of the surroundings, and he was proficient in the difficult art of creating gardens on slopes, as the gardens at Villa I Tatti (see page 132), Villa le Balze and Villa Capponi demonstrate.

At La Foce two garden styles meet. Cecil Pinsent was fascinated by the ideas of the Italian Renaissance garden with its geometrical forms, sightlines and viewing areas. It was necessary to create protection against *la cremontana* – the biting wind that sweeps in from the north-west in the autumn; without protection there was little prospect of plants surviving. Therefore Pinsent planted a wall of cypresses and hollies like a frame surrounding the garden. Inside were squares of box hedges defining garden rooms, as in Italian Renaissance gardens of the sixteenth and seventeenth centuries. From the house you look out along a box corridor nearly 100 metres (almost 330 feet) long, towards Mount Amiata in the distance. The box is clipped into hemispheres, whose small springy shiny leaves bounce back once touched. This is the main axis of the garden, from which the rooms are laid out. A pergola 75 metres (245 feet) long divides the garden into an upper and a lower part.

Next to the house is the Fountain Garden, an inner garden room enclosed by the L-shaped house. White and black tulips look up from inside the frame of box hedges, and in the middle is a rustic marble fountain. The Origos used local materials; all the stonework was made from porous marble quarried in the travertine caves outside Siena. In a corner of the Fountain Garden, dense bay laurel hedges forming a dome provided a hiding-place where Iris could sit and write in peace – one of many such writing places in the garden.

The Orangery is the largest garden room. The box hemispheres are repeated here at regular intervals. From the balustrade, I discover that the Lower Garden below is shaped like the bow of a ship. One of the magnificent magnolias has found itself stuck

Scarlet pelargoniums flourish in a great vase at the top of the stairs leading to the Lower Garden. The pergola behind is covered in wisteria.

when the roots have reached the rock below, and it has stopped growing. In a curtain of rigidly clipped cypresses, an opening has been left to provide a view of the valley. Another transverse axis starts in the middle of the Lemon Garden, stretching out across the slopes, past the stairs and the Rose Garden and up through a sloping avenue of cypresses, ending at a distant statue.

The way Cecil and Iris used the different heights to their advantage in order to create a garden with different levels is impressive. The inspiration for the upper flower garden comes from England and the Arts and Crafts movement – in particular the designs of Gertrude Jekyll. The conditions at La Foce are not as good as those in England but as well as the Rose Garden there are lavenders, peonies, anemones and geraniums, which flower in June through to July. The pergola is covered by old but thriving wisteria, all originating in one mother plant, its main stem almost as thick as a tree trunk. It is fast-growing but has a short flowering period. At the far end of the garden are herbs such as thyme, rosemary and sage, along with some Mediterranean shrubs.

On the slope above the long pergola is a bench with a somewhat blurred view across the undulating zigzag-shaped cypress avenue. I discover that Iris and Cecil were the creators behind the careful planting, or maybe it should be described as an art installation. The avenue was inspired by the frescoes of the fourteenth-century Sienese painter Ambrogio Lorenzetti.

In a subtly elegant way the garden gradually merges into the wilder countryside beyond. A path leads to a chapel and a tiny cemetery where the Origos' son Gianni is buried. He was only seven years old when he died.

Today, the estate owns the land all the way to San Quirico d'Orcia, and includes twenty-five farms. Some of the tenants of the farmhouses are farmers who lease the land; others are holidaymakers. The Origos bequeathed La Foce to their two daughters and several grandchildren. The younger daughter, Donata, lives abroad, so it is mainly Benedetta who spends time at La Foce, at weekends and during holidays. Benedetta is interested in the arts and every year she arranges cultural activities, garden courses and an annual chamber music festival (often at the end of July) in the village of Castelluccio. The concerts are held in churches, palaces and medieval towers in the area. Occasionally her son takes part as a cellist.

A CLASSIC TUSCAN GARDEN
DESIGNED FOR COSIMO I DE'MEDICI BY NICCOLÒ PERICOLI (KNOWN AS TRIBOLO) BEFORE 1550
COMPLETED BY GIORGIO VASARI 1567

Villa Castello

Florence

The Medici Villa Castello, three miles outside Florence, was probably the most important Tuscan garden of the Renaissance.

The Medici family had their origins in the countryside north-east of Florence. During the thirteenth century they left their farm in the Mugello valley in the Apennine mountains and moved to Florence in order to focus on trade and, later, banking. During the fifteenth and sixteenth centuries, the Medici built fifteen summer villas in total. In their quest for the right location for their villas they paid great attention to the writings of Antiquity and were particularly inspired by the letters of Pliny the Younger (see page 16), in which he talks about the importance of finding the *genius loci* – the soul of the place. The house and garden, Pliny writes, should be in harmony with the surrounding landscape. The climate and the environmental conditions such as compass points, winds, light and shade, heat and cold and access to water should be correct and in balance. At the same time spiritual criteria – mystical and magical dimensions – must also be fulfilled.

When Cosimo I de'Medici was elected Grand Duke of Tuscany in 1537, he commissioned a villa to be built in a village just outside Florence – the location of a Roman water reservoir (*castellum*) which gave the villa its name – with a garden based on designs by the sculptor and architect Niccolò Pericoli, also known as Tribolo.

An avenue of elm trees leads into the estate. Via a gate in the wall on the right-hand side you reach the garden, which is divided into three large terraces that climb upwards into the landscape.

The upper, wild part of the garden, the *bosco,* offers an allegorical portrayal of the Medici family's origins in the Apennine mountains. Among cypresses, oaks, holm oaks and meandering paths is a pond, where a giant shivering figure, a personification of

Opposite The main garden – on the lowest terrace – is laid out like a mathematical formula and consists of sixteen flower beds with a citrus tree in each corner. In its glory days, the garden at Villa Castello, rich with symbolism and plants, was considered perhaps the most beautiful garden in Europe. Today, it is famous for its many varieties of citrus tree.

The top terrace, the *bosco,* is dominated by mythology. In the middle of a pond surrounded by trees sits a man shivering and hugging himself. He personifies the Apennine mountains, from which the Medici family originated.

the Apennines, is hugging himself, trying to protect himself from the cold.

The middle terrace was created for lemon trees, and up until the end of the eighteenth century it was protected by a wall bordering the lower garden. During the nineteenth century, glasshouses were constructed to house the most tender plants. The glasshouses with big windows to the south serve the same purpose today, providing a shelter for the citrus trees during winter.

The main garden on the lowest terrace next to the house is made up of paths and sixteen rectangular flower beds inside box hedges. The hedges are accented by lemon and orange trees of every variety, planted in elaborately decorated terracotta pots on low pedestals. The inspiration for the terrace came largely from the rediscovered ideas of Antiquity and Hispano-Arabic gardens. The garden looks like a mathematical formula laid out in the untamed countryside. Expressing orderliness, conservatism and repetition, it clearly shows the desire of Renaissance man to control nature. Tribolo decorated the garden with specially commissioned statues representing various human virtues.

By great good fortune, the grotto below the top terrace, designed by Tribolo before 1550 and finished by Vasari in the 1560s, remains intact. Decorated with shells and differently coloured marble, it can be seen as the Renaissance answer to the nymphaea of Antiquity. It was created as a cool and shaded area where you could seek shelter from the sun and the heat. The ground is covered in black and white pebbles forming intricate patterns, and the roof is decorated with coloured shells. In her *Italian Villas and their Gardens* (1904), the American writer Edith Wharton describes the life-sized animals in the grotto as 'a camel, a monkey, a stag with real antlers, a wild boar with real tusks and various small animals and birds made of coloured marbles which correspond with their natural tints while beneath these groups are basins of pink and white marble, carved with sea-creatures and resting on dolphins.'

On your way into the grotto you might have been surprised by the unexpected *giochi d'acqua*. Water had great meaning for Cosimo de'Medici: it was a sign of wealth and prosperity, and a symbol of harmony. That is why he and Tribolo, who was a hydraulic engineer as well as an architect, built so many fountains of every kind in the garden at Villa Castello. An underground conduit brought water from the aqueducts, constructed by Tribolo especially for the garden, to the fountains and ponds.

The citrus trees are planted in urns which can be moved into glasshouses during the winter. Students and researchers come here to study the diverse collection of oranges and lemons. Every tree is carefully labelled with name and family.

Travel and the discovery of new continents enabled new and exotic plants to be brought to Europe, and Cosimo's gardener at Villa Castello ordered many foreign and rare plants. The orange trees came from Portugal, Naples, Genoa and Pietrasanta, and were cared for in movable urns. When travellers of the sixteenth and seventeenth centuries described Villa Castello as the most beautiful and opulent garden in Europe, they referred not just to the architecture and the fountains we can see today but also to the many exotic plants that grew there. Among these were pomegranates, climbing jasmines and espaliered Seville orange trees.

The garden at the Villa Castello took nearly forty years to build, and for much of that time the Duke was absorbed elsewhere. But in his later years he settled at the Villa Castello.

Towards the end of the eighteenth century, great changes took place in the garden, few for the better. The cypresses around the Hercules Fountain at the centre of the first terrace were removed, and the large fishponds in front of the house were filled in. Many of the rare and exotic plants died. No traces of the original planting remain, with the possible exception of a few trellised fruit trees along the walls.

Today, however, the garden has a rich collection of citrus trees, carefully labelled and numbered according to family and species. Students and botanists come here to study the plants.

A LONG STRAIGHT LINE

BAROQUE GARDEN DESIGNED BY CARLO FONTANA FOR CARDINAL FLAVIO CHIGI FROM 1680

ENGLISH GARDEN CREATED BY LORD LAMBTON IN THE TWENTIETH CENTURY

Villa Cetinale

Ancaiano

The ground and soil around Villa Cetinale is reddish-brown, rusty red, red as rowan berries in the autumn. It strikes me that there is an enormous difference in colour between Villa Cetinale and La Foce in Chianciano Terme, just twelve miles away. How can it be so different? Are there perhaps two versions of the *terra di Siena* pigment in the box of watercolours?

Designed in 1680 by the architect Carlo Fontana, the original garden layout is still there to be seen. The central axis, three miles long, starts somewhere far away in the landscape, passes through an avenue and ends on the summmit of a hill on the other side of the villa. Next to the historical part of the garden, the current owners, the Lambtons, have created an inviting English flower garden with roses and old-fashioned perennials.

Originally the house and the garden were created as a summer residence for Cardinal Flavio Chigi, nephew of Pope Alexander VII, on land once inhabited by the Etruscans. The Chigis, a banking and episcopal family, owned the villa until 1977, when they sold it to the British Lord Lambton. The house has been beautifully restored. On the ground floor is a wonderful entrance hall, where guests arriving by horse-drawn carriages were once greeted. On the upper floor, from large drawing rooms there are stunning views across the landscape and garden. There are three distinct garden areas, quite different from each other: the historical Baroque garden, the English flower garden and the Holy Wood, or *bosco*.

Carlo Fontana (1634–1714) was highly respected and versatile. He designed parts of St Peter's and various palaces in Rome, as well as the Borromeo Palace on Isola Bella (see page 184), and he often collaborated with Bernini. At Villa Cetinale it is easy to imagine him sitting at his desk with his pencil and ruler, confidently drawing a long

Above The immensely long main axis at Villa Cetinale runs through the house, along a lawn flanked by an avenue of cypresses, passing marble busts and obelisks, out into the landscape.

Opposite The silvery-blue border of aromatic plants such as lavender, cotton lavender, agapanthus and rosemary is flanked by a newly planted alley of cypresses. The pool glimmers in the background.

straight line through the undulating virgin landscape, to create that spectacular central axis.

Starting in the hills well to the south of Villa Cetinale, the axis passes a statue of Hercules, runs through the entrance gate – guarded by the Lambtons' dogs – and past a beautifully planted forecourt, then through the entrance hall of the house and out on the other side. It continues along a lawn flanked by an avenue of cypresses, passing marble busts and obelisks which are wedged in between the trees, until it reaches a terrace. Here it starts a steep ascent up the mountain, in the form of a rough staircase known as the Holy Staircase, or *Scala santa*, two hundred steps climbing up to a *romitorio*, or hermitage. Twelve monks are said to have lived here. They were provided with lodgings, books and furniture in return for caring for the sick and dying and keeping up a constant stream of prayer for the Pope and his family. From the *romitorio* one can admire the magnificent view of the hilly landscape of the Montagnola, across tiny houses and churches huddled together, forming their own little unit in the otherwise desolate landscape. The central axis of Villa Cetinale is probably the longest ever designed and built in Italy.

Back at the front of the villa, instead of walking through the house, I turn left after the box topiary and the lemon trees in terracotta urns. A gate is partly open. Beyond it is the English garden in the style of Gertrude Jekyll, or rather in the style of the Lambtons. The wall is covered in wisteria, which has nearly finished flowering; just a few odd blue racemes are hiding among the light, soft leaves. The hermitage is visible in the far distance, and in sharp contrast to the formal garden there are horses in paddocks stomping the reddish soil with their hooves. It is hot and dusty, and I hurry towards the shade of a rose pergola. I am surrounded by an abundance of flowers: roses, columbines, foxgloves

and delphiniums. Lord Lambton shows me a group of dark pink peonies next to a topiary box figure. This part of the garden is divided into flower beds separated by paths, with rose pergolas at the intersections. Butterflies jostle for food in a long silvery-blue border with lavender, cotton lavender and other silver-leaved plants. At the far end of the path there is a turquoise glimmer: the water of the swimming pool, which looks tempting in the heat. Lord Lambton talks about his plans for developing this area of the garden and draws on a piece of paper. We are surrounded by circular fences which support trellised pear trees. There are also many yew trees clipped into sugarloaf shapes.

I turn a key in a lock and enter the Holy Wood. Beyond a gate is a forested area with paths, glades and an enchanting lake, surrounded by a circular pathway that was once used for hunting and horse racing. At the end of the tiny paths are seven little chapels decorated with faded frescoes and covered in moss. Magical and spooky, the wood is encircled by a perimeter wall approximately three miles long. For twenty years, at the end of the seventeenth and the beginning of the eighteenth centuries, the great Sienese horse race known as the Palio was held here because of riots in Siena.

Villa Cetinale is a successful combination of new and old. The Lambtons have kept Carlo Fontana's brave garden plan alive, while at the same time putting their own personal stamp on it with the English flower garden.

Above
Left One of the many pergolas, weighed down by an abundance of roses.
Right In the English garden, box topiary figures mingle with pink peonies.

Opposite The axis runs straight through the estate, up to the Hermitage at the top of the Holy Staircase.

A BAROQUE BALLROOM AND A GREEN THEATRE

Created for the Orsetti Family in the Seventeenth Century
Landscape Garden and Restoration of Italian Gardens by Jacques Greber for Count and Countess Pecci-Blunt from 1923

Villa Reale

Lucca

Napoleon's sister had made up her mind. Now that she was Princess of Lucca she wanted a home that matched her position – a beautiful villa worthy of a royal personage. It should be a country estate with a Baroque garden, similar to that of the French palace at Versailles but smaller. She settled for Villa Reale in Marlia near Lucca. The owners, the Orsetti family, who had owned the estate for 150 years, vacated the property. Whether they left voluntarily is not known. This is said to be how Elisa Baciocchi acquired Villa Reale in 1806.

Lucca is one of the most beautiful of all Italian towns, a medieval gem built on a Roman street plan and surrounded by a beautiful and well-preserved perimeter wall. To the north-east is a scenic rural landscape, where there are a number of villas. In the village of Marlia is Villa Reale, the grandest of them all.

The wall surrounding the garden is fifteen miles long – the same length as Lucca's town wall. Beyond an avenue of plane trees a wide open lawn stretches out in front of the building like a theatrical stage. Hiding behind trees and perfectly clipped hedges is a series of beautiful garden rooms, including the Lemon Garden with its fishpond, the Green Theatre (*teatro di verdura*), the Spanish Garden, the Water Theatre behind the palace and the Camellia Walk.

The layout of the garden is difficult to take in, as it is in two distinct styles. Most of the garden rooms were originally laid out for the Orsetti in the seventeenth century. When Count and Countess Pecci-Blunt bought the estate in 1923, they commissioned French architect Jacques Greber to work on the garden. Alongside the existing Italian gardens, he created a romantic landscape garden with shrubs, streams and wooded areas. The garden is criss-crossed by footpaths, but there is no continuous walk.

Above The Spanish Garden looks as if it were inspired by the water channels of the Alhambra.

Opposite Along the Camellia Walk the camellia bushes seem to grow almost wild beside the stream, surrounded by mosses, ivy and laurels.

The Green Theatre, or *teatro di verdura*. Clipped trees and bushes form a theatre complete with a stage, lights, prompt box and space for the audience. Waiting in the wings, in niches, are figures from the *Commedia dell'Arte* tradition: Columbine, Pantalone and Pulcinella, all made of terracotta.

Many of the garden rooms are very well kept; others have an air of faded beauty about them. Fifty years ago the owner employed at least thirty gardeners but today there are only four. The head gardener, Mr Pietro Serafini, came here as a teenager in the 1950s. He tells me that back then the owners wanted different flowers each season throughout the year. This is no longer the case, but the garden had a major facelift during the 1990s with extensive restorations.

We stand at the top of Montagnola, a small hill in the middle of the great lawn, looking out across the many elegant trees in the park: firs, oaks, cedars of Lebanon, thujas and the oriental plane trees (*Platanus orientalis*) that were planted in great numbers in the eighteenth century by a previous owner, the Spanish Princess Maria Luisa of Bourbon, who became Duchess of Lucca. At the bottom of the lawn there is a lake, where a lone swan is swimming in splendid isolation. He does not seem to like the noise from our cameras, so he heads for the shore and dry land, hissing. We run. Church bells are ringing.

The Camellia Walk is perhaps the most delightful part of the garden. A slow stream of water is surrounded by camellias in full bloom. There are many varieties, since camellias hybridize easily. One specimen with exquisite snow-white flowers with the palest pink streaks stands next to another with intense pink petals framing yellow spots in the centre. When I finally manage to take my eyes off the beautiful petals floating in the water, I discover some evergreen periwinkle (*Vinca major*) on the ground, along with some wild blue violas, a bamboo copse and laurel trees. There is

The fishpond with its decorative balustrade and lemon trees has been compared to 'a baroque ballroom'. The surrounding trees are reflected in the shining 'floor', which is graced by an elegant (but bad-tempered) swan.

also a holly – a rare tree in this part of Europe – which has self-seeded here from the Pisano mountains.

Near the house is the Lemon Garden, with the fishpond described by Georgina Masson in *Italian Gardens* as 'surely the most magnificent in Italy'. It 'calls to mind some vast baroque ballroom whose dancing floor is a great sheet of shimmering water. In this are reflected the dark clipped yews and lighter greens of the "walls", the grey stone of the balustrades and presiding gods and goddesses and, like so many little lamps, the golden fruit of the potted orange and lemon trees.' A fountain throws a jet of water high into the air. As I look at it there is a slight breeze and some droplets fall on the visitors and the marble statues.

Beyond the gate are two secret pergolas, but I decide to head straight on towards the most interesting of all the garden rooms. The Green Theatre, or *teatro di verdura*, is a complete theatre, with vegetation forming the walls, the scenery and the stage lights. There is even a prompt box. The theatre looks as if it has recently been trimmed: a wooden ladder has been left on the scene. Waiting in the wings are terracotta actors depicting Columbine, Pantalone and Pulcinella, all characters of the *Commedia dell'Arte*.

If the heat gets too intense, you could head for the Grotto of Pan. Some of the building materials are by-products from the iron industry of the sixteenth and seventeenth centuries. The water jets under the stone flooring are still working. This was a place for *al fresco* dinners and the room above was probably a perfect place for romantic meetings.

DROUGHT-RESISTANT AROMATIC PLANTS IN SOUTHERN TUSCANY
DESIGNED BY DON LEEVERS AND LINDSAY MEGARRITY FROM 1988

Venzano

Volterra

Above A rickety vine pergola frames the view over the barren landscape 'at the end of the road' near Volterra in southern Tuscany. The colour of the hills changes with the seasons, from green in spring via brown and gold to grey in August, and then back to green again.

Opposite Spring offers an abundance of beautiful blooms in the flower beds below the house, then the drought-tolerant plants come into their own during summer. The overall structure of the garden is visible throughout the year, in the shape of trees, hedges, pergolas and walls.

I have never seen a landscape like this before. Surely nothing can grow here without irrigation? But in fact the idea of Don Leevers and Lindsay Megarrity, who have created a home and a garden here, is to grow and sell plants that can withstand the hot and dry Tuscan climate.

The scenic road SP68 leads towards the sea, flanked by soft hills and cypresses, which are like black markers along the road. Halfway between Volterra and Colle Val d'Elsa is a sign saying 'Mazzolla'. The landscape is desolate but very beautiful.

Some time during the thirteenth century, a group of Augustinian monks reached this 'godforsaken place' at the end of the road – Venzano means 'in the middle of nowhere'. On the site of an earlier Etruscan settlement there was a freshwater spring, which gave them the means of survival, and they decided to stop. They built a church and the place became a working monastery where wine, olives and fruit were produced.

In 1988, Don Leevers and Lindsay Megarrity, garden designers and plantsmen from Australia, came across Venzano. They had a dream: they wanted to create a nursery in order to help customers make their own gardens, and show that it is possible to have a beautiful flowering garden in Tuscany with plants that can survive without regular watering.

'It is a new thing to create a garden here,' says Don. 'We wanted to give people the confidence to be daring. Traditionally, people have had no leisure time or money, but things are changing. People travel a lot more, and they are becoming more interested.'

The garden is in front of the house, facing the valley. Small garden rooms are protected by hedges and walls, which help the plants survive the freezing Tramontana

Don, who is also a geologist, built the beautiful wall himself. A variety of Mexican daisy (*Erigeron karvinskianus*) has self-seeded in the cracks. In the background is a dense laurel hedge.

wind in wintertime. In the corners grow bulbous plants such as irises and gladioli, which Don and Lindsay hope will survive without being eaten by porcupines, who are rather keen on bulbs. In a semi-shaded area outside a little chapel, potted plants are for sale. From every part of the garden, there is a panoramic view of the valley to the south, in all its glory. It is like an ever-changing work of art, where the colours vary according to the growing season: green, brown and gold in August, grey and then green again.

Among the herbs for sale at Venzano, rosemary is one of the specialities and forty varieties can be found here. Rosemary thrives in the hot, dry climate and some flower from September through to May. A pretty pink one is *Rosmarinus* 'Vicomte de Noailles', which was discovered in the Atlas Mountains in Morocco. A rosemary with tiny little leaves and pale blue flowers is known as *R.* 'Gethsemane'. *R.* 'Jackman's Prostratus' is very compact and has dark blue flowers. 'Occasionally we discover new varieties, which have cross-bred on the wall, and if they are beautiful and interesting in some way we give them a new name,' Don explains.

Salvia, thyme, oregano, basil, mint, hyssops and several varieties of lavender also thrive in this almost subtropical climate. *Lavandula angustifolio* 'Hidcote Blue' and 'Hidcote Pink' are listed in Venzano's plant catalogue, along with *L.* 'Munstead', *L.* 'Twickel Purple', the larger *L.* x *intermedia* 'Grappenhall', and *L. lanata* 'Venzano', a robust hybrid with silvery-grey leaves and blue flowers.

The plants at Venzano are mainly Mediterranean, but also come from Australia, South America, Africa, the Canary Islands, Asia, the Pyrenees, the Himalayas and California. From Europe there are also lily of the valley (*Convallaria majalis*), the fragrant sweet violet (*Viola odorata*), bulbous plants like the pink *Allium schoenoprasum* and the white *A. triquetrum,* a fine-scented

Geranium viscosissimum (pinky-purple flowers) and many varieties of wormwood: *Artemisia camphorata* (grey leaves and yellow flowers), *A. absinthum* (evergreen with silvery-green leaves and tiny flowers) and *A. pontica* (silvery-green leaves and yellow flowers). Irises of many kinds also thrive in the Tuscan climate. We stop by the Florentine iris (*I. florentina*), which is white with a tinge of pale blue.

'In twenty years' time I'm sure there will be some very interesting gardens in Tuscany,' says Don. 'Most Italians want to import concepts from England: they want to have a rose garden, a lawn and irrigation. I think that is silly because at the end of the day our style is beautiful.'

Climbing up the walls of the house is *Rosa* 'Cooperi', which has an interesting story, as Don explains: 'The climbing rose originates from a seed in the botanical garden in Rangoon. A Mr Cooper sent it to Dublin's botanical gardens. It is very drought-tolerant and has reached the roof several times and covered two rooms. It is one of few roses which keep their leaves throughout the winter.'

A farmer, Franco, leases the farmland on the lower terrace. He grows vegetables, which he shares with Don and Lindsay. Franco also makes wine (undrinkable, according to Don) from the black and white grapes that grow up the pergola. Further up along the path are huge pomegranate trees, which Don describes as 'our treasure'. They are three or four hundred years old. There is also a Chinese date tree (*Ziziphus jujuba*), which bears fruits that taste at first like apples but more like dates when ripe. It is the last tree to lose its leaves.

Beyond the valley, in the distance, lies Volterra on a hill. In the evening you can wander along the path that leads nowhere, accompanied by billions of fireflies dancing in the air. It is an enchanted place, and for nearly a thousand years people have been happy here at the end of the road.

Drought-resistant plants readily self-seed at Venzano, forming soft cushions in the gravel. The cream-coloured flowers are a variety of Californian puppy called *Eschscholzia californica*. Other plants found in the gravel are rosemary, phlomis, thyme and lavender.

A BALANCED ECOLOGY
DESIGNED BY PIETRO PORCINAI IN THE TWENTIETH CENTURY

Above The garden of Villa Martello reaches out into the surrounding landscape.

Opposite At Villa La Terrazza in Florence, the pool is shaped in an imaginative and playful way, so that it blends softly into the garden greenery.

Gardens by Pietro Porcinai

Around Florence

Pietro Porcinai was probably the most productive and the most influential Italian landscape architect of the twentieth century. He designed not only private gardens but also public parks, motorway areas and holiday villages. He was also commissioned to improve the areas around both new and old factories. He was passionately devoted to the ideal of creating a more human working environment through the use of plants, light and water.

The son of Martino Porcinai, who restored the Renaissance garden at Villa Gamberaia (see page 102), Pietro was born at Villa Gamberaia in 1910. He was particularly influenced by his father's water parterre, and used it as an inspiration in various of his own designs over the years.

Pietro was an inquisitive and intelligent boy, and as an eleven-year-old received a grant to study horticulture and garden architecture. Later, after studying in Florence, he went to Germany, Belgium and Holland to learn more of garden architecture. As Italy became more prosperous in the years after the Second World War, he was inundated by commissions, mainly from wealthy Italians and Germans who wanted help with their private villa gardens. Pietro's basic idea was that the clients should play a major part in creating their own gardens, and that the role of the landscape architect was to offer advice and answer queries about what plants could survive in a particular environment. The most important thing was to start with the existing landscape and choose plants of a similar type in order to achieve balance and beauty.

Through a gate on a meandering street in Fiesole lies a beautiful example of the private gardens designed by Pietro Porcinai. From the terrace of Villa Il Martello, you

can see the valley below. On the slope down towards Florence is an olive grove. The transition from well-kept garden to open landscape is almost unnoticeable: everything blends together as a unit. The silver colour of the leaves of the olive trees is reflected in a planting of silvery and steely-grey plants, including cotton lavender (*Santolina chamaecyparissus*), germander (*Teucrium divaricatum*), lavender (*Lavandula angustifolia*), bush germander (*Teucrium fruticans*) and dark green mahonia. Contrast is offered by red leadwort (*Plumbago indica*) and by groups of blue forget-me-nots, in buried pots. The swimming pool at the bottom of the garden is invisible until you are very close. It is surrounded by olive trees and terracotta tiles, and the view of Brunelleschi's Duomo is breathtaking. The garden has an airy and natural feel, despite the fact that all the details and the planting have been carefully planned.

In Pietro Porcinai's projects, certain common themes emerge: the garden as an extension of the landscape; strong forms and geometrical shapes; respect for nature and an ecological balance. He described his work as 'the healing of the landscape', and spoke of how 'You must feel how the earth breathes when you touch it and have a patient respect for nature.'

ORDER AND UNITY IN A MEDICI VILLA
DESIGNED BY DAVIDE FORTINI FOR COSIMO I DE'MEDICI 1550
COMPLETED BY RAFFAELLO PAGNI FOR FERDINANDO DE'MEDICI 1591–9

Villa Petraia

Florence

A short walk from Villa Castello (see page 112) lies Villa Petraia. It was designed in 1550 by Davide Fortini for Cosimo I, and later finished by Raffaello Pagni, who also designed the garden, on the instructions of Cosimo's son, the Grand Duke Ferdinando de'Medici, creator of Villa Castello (see page 112). Villa Petraia sits high up on a hill with panoramic views across the landscape. The formal garden in front of the house is made up of three terraces – two narrow ones, linked by staircases, and one long and gently sloping. It includes a parterre made up of box hedge patterns filled with different plants, mainly irises; and in front of the house is a decorative pool with glassy water – a fishpond that is in fact a tank which supplies the garden with plenty of water. Behind the villa is an English landscape garden. If you follow the pond to the left, you come to an area with flowers and lemon trees. The hothouse here was built in 1833 to protect the tropical plants which were fashionable at the time. Today, a line of citrus trees in urns sends out wafts of glorious scent through the open windows. Victor Emmanuel, the first king of the united Italy, owned the villa from 1872. The loggia that he created by covering a mid-sixteenth-century courtyard with a glass dome is well worth a visit.

Above The pool on the terrace below the house is a water tank which supplies the whole garden. A staircase leads up to the entrance and the beautiful loggia of Victor Emmanuel. The views from here across the plain of the Arno and the distant mountains are impressive.

Opposite The Villa Petraia has a tower which is strikingly similar to that of Palazzo Vecchio in Florence. On the slope in front of the house is a parterre of box hedges forming patterns which are filled with a variety of plants, mainly irises.

A MODERN INTERPRETATION OF A RENAISSANCE GARDEN

Created by Cecil Pinsent in Collaboration with Geoffrey Scott from 1909

Above A modern parterre laid out in a geometrical pattern. The spaces between the low box hedges are filled with cotton lavender, creating a striking contrast between the silvery grey and the green.

Opposite The main garden is laid out on a slope, with a long central axis surrounded by a repeated pattern. Cecil Pinsent, who was very interested in mathematics, had a penchant for trimming topiary into geometrical shapes.

Villa I Tatti

Settignano

In 1909 the new owners of Villa I Tatti, art historian Bernard Berenson and his wife Mary, commissioned British architect Cecil Pinsent to redesign the existing farmhouse and orchard, and create a formal garden on the adjacent slope that looks towards the Arno valley. It was Pinsent's first major architectural project, to be followed by many more in Tuscany, such as La Foce (see page 108), Villa Medici and Le Balze in Fiesole. From 1914 his compatriot Geoffrey Scott, author of *The Architecture of Humanism*, collaborated in the work at Villa I Tatti.

Pinsent had studied the structure and proportions of Renaissance gardens and wanted to convey their atmosphere and flavour at Villa I Tatti. He saw nearby Villa Gamberaia (see page 102) as the perfect garden model, summarizing his observations of it in 1931: 'The garden must give us the impression that the house is laid out in the open air and its various aspects must reveal themselves one by one so that, in passing through, one experiences a varied series of impressions.'

He started systematically by creating a framework and basis for the garden in the shape of walls, staircases and new avenues of trees. Then he created separate garden rooms on the different terraces surrounding the house.

Today Villa I Tatti is very well kept and a pleasure to explore. The smaller garden rooms are filled with plants framed by lush box hedges forming patterns. On a wall are beautiful branches of wisteria that are almost a work of art in themselves. The Italian Garden, which is made up of rectangles, clipped box pyramids and intricate pebblestone paths, gradually blends into a wilder area where nature has been helped along and a landscape of meadows, streams and flowering fruit trees spreads out on the slope. Villa I Tatti offers one of the best examples of combined formality and informality, a modern interpretation of the gardens of the Renaissance and Antiquity.

MODERN MAGIC

Designed by Niki de Saint Phalle 1979–96

The Tarot Garden

Garavicchio

Opposite Of this figure, Niki de Saint Phalle wrote: 'I made the card of *The Empress* my home and she became the centre of the garden. It was here the crew ate my meals and made the models for the remaining cards. I lived alone in the Sphinx, which is what we nicknamed *The Empress*. Total immersion was the only way to realize the garden.'

The Tarot Garden is a modern sculpture park by the artist Niki de Saint Phalle, who, with the help of friends, colleagues and craftsmen, created twenty giant sculptures based on the main tarot cards. Each figure has a specific meaning and significance. It is without doubt a most unusual place.

The low evening sun is reflected in the mirrors and tiles that decorate the sculptures. Seeing these works of art in a natural environment is an experience that is beyond description. It makes you think that anything is possible. Inside an eight-headed dragon, a man is hanging upside down, his orange hair falling down towards the mirrors. This is card number XII, *The Hanged Man*, representing compassion. A bird from the legends of Native Americans and Mexicans flies close to the sun; its wings of red, orange and green tiles reach up to the treetops. This is card number XIX, *The Sun*. Through the bird's dark blue tiled legs I can see something very strange in the distance: parts of a giant female. This is card number III, *The Empress*, Niki's most important figure.

A thousand questions demand answers. It is said that one of Niki de Saint Phalle's main sources of inspiration was the Park Guell in Barcelona by the Catalan artist Antoni Gaudí. It is possible that she was also influenced by the 'monsters' in the Renaissance park of Bomarzo (see page 44), which is not all that far from here. But how were the sculptures made? Who fired the tiles? Who polishes all the tiles and mirrors? A man who looks very much at home here is moving around among crooked columns decorated with colourful tiles – they look like liquorice allsorts but are in fact glazed ceramics. He is Rico Weber, who together with the artists Jean Tinguely and Seppi Imhof formed the first crew when *The Empress*, *The High Priestess* and *The Magician* were built. He tells me how they sprayed cement on to frames of welded steel bars and

chicken wire, and how local craftsmen were involved in the firing of the ceramic tiles. Rico talks about Stockholm in the late 1960s, where he first met Niki and they created their first giant sculpture, *She*, for Moderna Museet (at the time run by Pontus Hultén). In the Tarot Garden Niki de Saint Phalle's dream of giant statues in a 'garden of joy' finally came true; she was able to see her life's work completed before she died.

THE CITY PARK OF FLORENCE

ORIGINAL DESIGN BY NICCOLÒ PERICOLI (KNOWN AS TRIBOLO) FOR ELEANOR OF TOLEDO 1549

The Boboli Gardens

Florence

The Boboli Gardens lie behind Palazzo Pitti in Florence, where today they form the city's park. When Cosimo de'Medici's wife, Eleanor of Toledo, bought the estate from the Pitti family in 1549, she commissioned Tribolo, who was already working at Villa Castello (see page 112) to design the gardens. By the summer of 1550 Tribolo was dead, but, according to his contemporary Giorgio Vasari in *Lives of the Artists,* he had in less than a year designed the whole layout of the hill behind the palace and the planting of the *boschi*.

The gardens were substantially enlarged in the seventeenth century, and it was then that the central axis demarcated by the Cypress Avenue, or *Viottolone*, was laid out. A stroll along the Cypress Avenue takes you to the serene and beautiful Island Pond, or *Isolotto.* Created by Alfonso Parigi in 1614, this room is based on the Maritime Theatre at Hadrian's Villa. In the middle is the jewel in the Boboli crown: an oval basin with a small island in the centre. Here stands the Fountain of the Ocean by Giambologna (1550), with Neptune and other sea gods below representing the Nile, the Ganges and the Euphrates. Statues of other mythological figures, including Perseus and Andromeda, rise out of the water. Up some steps is the Knight's Garden, or *Giardino del Cavaliere.* In May the terrace is full of flowering peonies as well as Banksian, Tea and Bourbon roses. The view of farmland and medieval towers gives you an idea of what the landscape south of the Arno would have looked like before the fifteenth century. On your way out you will pass the great Amphitheatre, where the Medici family staged plays and entertainments.

Top The Cypress Avenue, planted in 1614, forms the main axis of the Boboli Gardens. The niches hold Classical statues, many of them copies of Roman originals.
Middle Rising out of the water of the Island Pond are statues of mythological figures, including the white marble Andromeda by Giovan Battista Pieratti.
Bottom The horseshoe-shaped Amphitheatre, built in a natural valley behind the palace, looks like a Roman hippodrome. The lawn is surrounded by seating for the audience, niches with statues and tightly pruned trees.

Parco di Demidoff

Pratolino

Parco di Demidoff is a lovely place to stroll around in, even though its original layout was lost in 1830. Once known as Villa Medici Pratolino, it was designed by architect Bernardo Buontalenti between 1569 and 1581 for Francesco I de'Medici and was a great formal garden famous for its grottoes, fountains and water jokes. Today, the estate is owned by the Demidoff family, who have restored parts of the garden. Many footpaths snake their way through the 75-acre park. Beyond the welcoming avenue is a group of statues: mythological figures that climb out of the earth in a meadow full of buttercups. The main attraction of the park – both in the past and today – is Giambologna's *Colosso dell'Appennino* (1579).

Villa Mansi

Segromigno

The garden of the Villa Mansi was originally laid out in the eighteenth century in a French style by Filippo Juvarra, but it was later transformed into a romantic English landscape garden. In the copse a short distance from the house I am surprised by an irregularly shaped pool which looks like a small forest lake among the trees. The elegant statues surrounding it give a hint of what the garden might have looked like during its French period. There is both a formal and a magical feeling to the place. Instead of a traditional grotto, a scene depicting the bath of Diana has been created next to a group of flowering camellias: Diana is assisted by a nymph as she bathes in a lake, while a man looks on.

Villa Garzoni

Collodi

The village of Collodi is dominated by the faded beauty of the Baroque garden of Villa Garzoni, created in 1756 by the architect Ottavio Diodati. A succession of terraces planned symmetrically around a central axis is laid out against the hillside. Between two ponds at the lowest level are box topiary shapes and wavy cypress hedges. Above is the water staircase, from which you can continue by footpaths to a maze and a green open-air theatre formed by trees and plants. The house, a formal palace, is further up at the edge of the park, which is unusual in a Baroque setting.

Villa Vicobello

Siena

The Villa Vicobello is thought to have been designed by Baldassare Peruzzi (1480–1536), who was a contemporary of Raphael and a pupil of Bramante. The son of a poor weaver, Baldassare was born in the tiny village of Ancaiano west of Siena; however, he was baptized in Siena and became known as Baldassare da Siena. Early recognition of his enormous talent as an artist and an architect brought him to the centre of power in Rome, where he undertook many commissions, including work at St Peter's.

The terraced garden at Vicobello is on a south-facing slope and has a view across the medieval city of Siena and the cathedral dome. It is mainly in the classic Italian tradition, with parterres of box hedge filled with grasses or plants and punctuated by trimmed hemispheres and other topiary shapes typical of the sixteenth century. The terraces are decorated with urns of orange and lemon trees, and wherever you look you will find the coat of arms, depicting six mountains, of the Chigi family – the villa's owners. The western part of Vicobello is wilder and planted with horse chestnuts and hollies. This area is known as the English Wood.

The Carla Fineschi Rose Garden

Cavriglia

Professor Gianfranco Fineschi, the most passionate rose collector in Tuscany – perhaps even in the world – has dedicated the past thirty years to work on the Carla Fineschi botanical rose garden in Cavriglia outside Arezzo. The garden has been open to the public since the late 1990s. It is laid out rather like a library of the world's roses, or a living museum, with roses planted according to botanical classification, and labels on each rose specifying name, year of introduction to Europe and often breeding history. As many as 6,500 roses are on display, one plant of each variety. As an extra touch, peacocks strut around among the flowers.

Villa Vignamaggio

Greve di Chianti

The Renaissance Villa Vignamaggio, now run as a country hotel, is located in the Chianti wine district between Florence and Siena. Immediately to the south of Greve, a tiny road snakes its way towards the village of Lamole. Beyond a hairpin bend, the house, with its subtle hues of ochre pink, comes into view at the top of the hill, 350 metres (1150 feet) above the sea.

The villa is mainly south-facing, with views across olive groves and vineyards. At the back is an Italian garden in the traditional style, with hedges forming decorative patterns, broken by hemispheres of clipped box. Large urns with colourful plants stand out against the ochre-coloured walls. If, like the actors in the 1993 film of *Much Ado about Nothing*, which was set here, you dance further into the garden, you end up in the cypress avenue.

Vignamaggio is also said to have been the birthplace of Mona Lisa Gherardini, later Lisa del Giocondo – Leonardo's Mona Lisa.

The Iris Garden

Florence

In Florence's Piazzale Michelangelo lies a garden dedicated to the iris – the symbol of Florence since the thirteenth century. The entrance is to the right of the eastern terrace of the piazza and the garden stretches far down the slope towards the River Arno. It is a lovely, peaceful place, very different from the western terrace of the piazza, where tourists gather for the view. The Iris Garden is run by the Società Italiana dell'Iris (SIDI) and more than 2,500 varieties of iris flower here among olive trees. The SIDI organizes an annual iris flower show during three weeks in May.

VENETO

ITALY'S OLDEST BOX PARTERRE

CREATED FOR AGOSTINO GIUSTI FROM ABOUT 1570

Giardino Giusti

Verona

Unhappy love and Shakespeare – when you think of Verona, you associate the town not just with its famous Arena opera stage but also with great theatrical dramas. Shakespeare's *Romeo and Juliet* is set here, and the famous balcony of the play can be found in the historical quarter.

I head east from the centre and cross the River Ádige, to find the Giusti Gardens behind the Palazzo Giusti. The façade of the palace is squeezed in an old Roman street in a lively part of the town, where many water mills were once located. The first thing to catch my eye on entering the garden is a white marble statue of a seated Venus, the Roman goddess of love and beauty. She is one of many statues of mythological figures in the garden, including Bacchus and Mercury. Other statues symbolize the ideal pursuits of the Renaissance, such as poetry and philosophy, and reflect the interest of the Giusti in humanist culture.

The Giusti family came to Verona in the early fourteenth century from Tuscany. The family was involved in the wool trade and one branch, who later took the name of Giusti del Giardino (the Giusti of the Garden), became important contributors to the cultural life of Verona. Agostino Giusti, Knight of the Venetian Republic and Squire of the Grand Duke of Tuscany, was something of a politician and intellectual leader in sixteenth-century Verona. As the owner of the palace, he was the man behind the original plan of the garden.

The surrounding wall of the garden is crowned by a repeated decorative pattern known, after the city, as 'Verona', with crenellations reminiscent of the spikes of a royal crown. From the gateposts, which are topped by two obelisks, an avenue of tall cypresses forming the central axis of the garden leads the eye to the steep hillside of San Zeno in Monte and a grotto carved out of tufa. The grotto is now derelict, but

Pages 140–41 The square building of Villa Capra, 'La Rotonda', designed in 1567 by Andrea Palladio. Standing on a small hill in the fertile landscape above Vicenza, the villa commands extensive views on all sides over the gardens and the surrounding farmland.

Opposite In 1570, Agostino Giusti, a Veronese man of culture, created a garden behind his palace. The current owners, Counts Justo and Nicolò Giusti, are trying to keep the garden true to its original design.

1 Alley of cypresses
2 Parterres (originally flanked by tall cypresses)
3 Maze
4 Stone mask and balcony
5 Cave

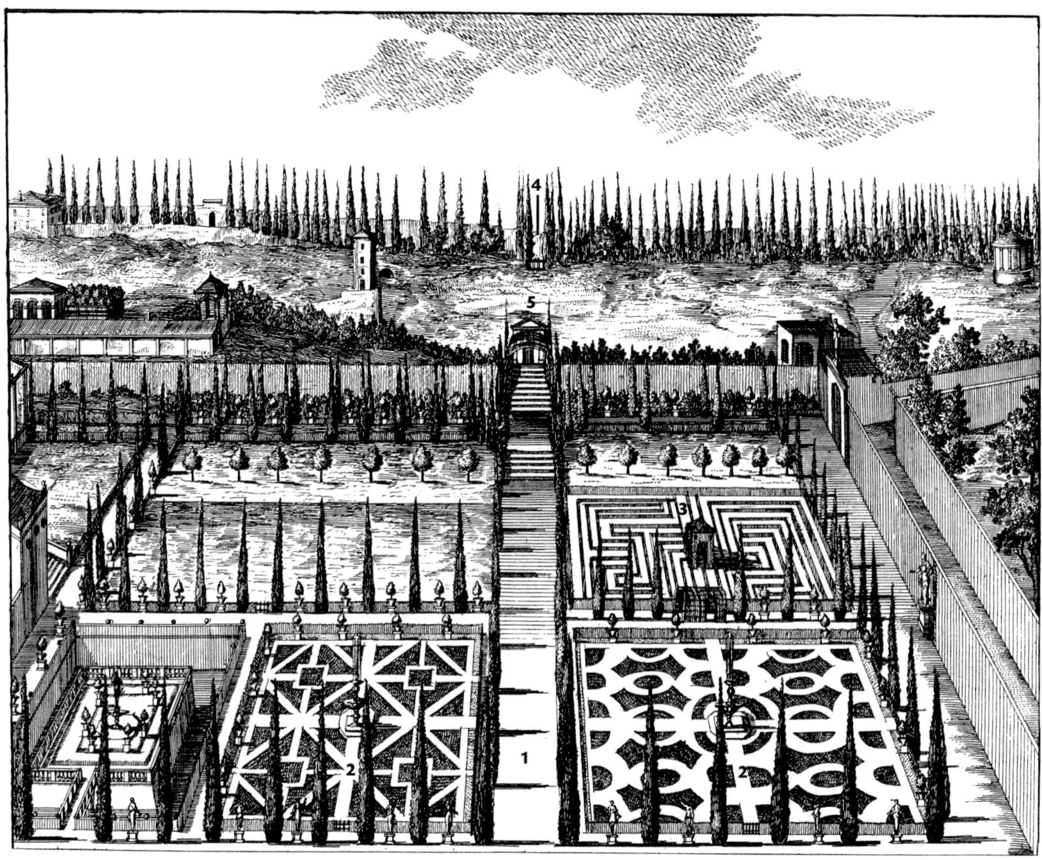

Plan of the Giusti gardens, drawn by J.C. Volkamer in 1714. Despite alterations in the eighteenth century, in the then fashionable English landscape style, the basic layout of the garden is the same today as it was in the sixteenth century.

it was once decorated with mirrors, shells and water features; the distorting play of mirrors was meant to confuse visitors, and symbolize the contrast between reason and the horrors and magic of nature. Above the grotto, halfway up the hillside, is a giant stone mask and behind is a small room where they used to light fires that would emerge through the mouth of the mask. The garden is laid out on different rising levels, and from the top of the hill there is a stunning view of Verona.

Giardino Giusti was one of the sites usually included in the Grand Tour, a trip taken from the sixteenth century onwards by many young aristocrats and artists to learn about the cultural treasures of Europe. They often arrived in Italy via the Brenner Pass, and Verona – a junction between northern Italy and the rest of Europe – was a natural stopping point.

The French scholar Charles de Brosses, President of the Parliament of Burgundy, mentions Giardino Giusti in 1739: 'The Giusti gardens gave me more pleasure; they are filled with rocky landscapes, grottoes and endless terraces covered with small circular temples.' Having described the cypresses, he continues: 'I found myself lost in a maze and walked around for a whole hour in the hot sunshine. I would probably still be there, if a gardener hadn't helped me find my way out.'

The German poet Goethe visited here while he was living in Rome, and a cypress just inside the gate is named after him. He is supposed to have sat under this tree while writing some of the essays that he would publish in *Italian Journey* (*1786–88*),

the diary of his Grand Tour. He describes the Giusti Gardens as beautifully situated, with 'monstrous' cypresses, and recounts how he made a bouquet of caper flowers from the garden and then went into town carrying it, 'to the astonishment of the Veronese people'.

In the nineteenth century the Giardino Giusti were transformed into landscape gardens. During the last part of the twentieth century, however, the site was restored by Counts Justo and Nicolò Giusti to close to its original layout. They have researched the historical records and have tried to restore the beautiful lower terrace and the parterres to their authentic state.

The maze is believed to be one of the oldest in Europe, with the same pattern as designed in 1796 by Luigi Trezza, an architect from Verona. It has recently been replanted, but it will be a few years before the hedges are tall enough for anyone to get lost in it again.

March – early in the season – is a good time to visit the garden, as most of the trees are free from leaves then and the box parterre can be seen perfectly from the top of the hill. The parterre is said to be the oldest in Italy, although there is no firm evidence to that effect. The stroll up the hill from the parterre, by way of the stone stairs, is eased by an eighteenth-century garden pavilion halfway up. Here you can rest and study the garden and the delightfully formed parterre. From the top of the hill, the views across Verona are breathtaking, and if you have twenty-twenty vision you will be able to glimpse the Roman elliptical amphitheatre, the Arena.

Right
Top The cypress avenue starts at the entrance gate and follows a straight line to the steep slope of San Zeno in Monte. From the belvedere there are breathtaking views across Verona, and you realize just how small the people are compared to the tall and ancient cypresses.
Middle Detail of the garden, showing a geometric box hedge design. Agostino Giusti's interest in humanist culture is reflected in the statues, which symbolize the ideals of the Renaissance in their representation of philosophers and mythological figures.
Bottom As you ascend the stone stairs, there are several landings on which you can stop and catch your breath – and at the same time admire the stone decorations and the parterre, which is best seen from above.

THE CIRCULAR BOTANICAL GARDEN
CREATED FROM 1545

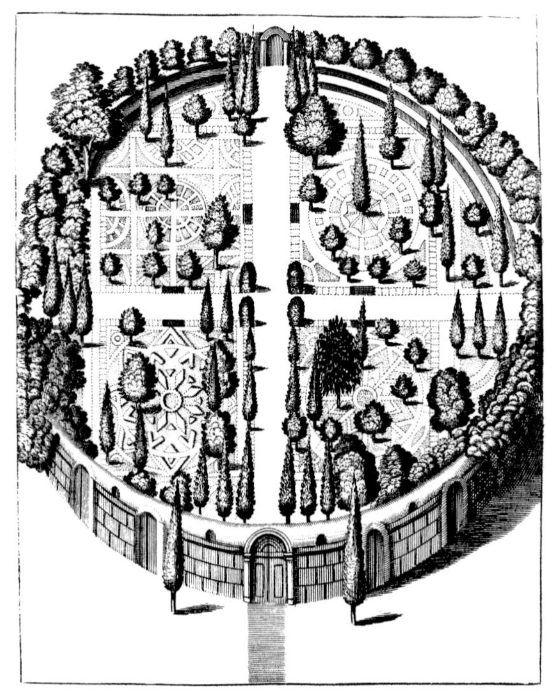

A plan from 1654 by Tomasini of the Orto Botanico in Padua. The circular area has a diameter of 84 metres (275 feet). Archaeological investigation has revealed that the basic layout of the garden is more or less the same today as when it was first created in 1545.

Orto Botanico
Padua

The Orto Botanico is a gem in the heart of old Padua, just a stone's throw from the impressive Sant'Antonio basilica with its Oriental-inspired domes. Created in 1545, it is one of the world's earliest university botanical gardens and the oldest example in which the original layout survives almost unchanged. Since 1997, Orto Botanico has been included in the UNESCO World Heritage List.

The garden was started by Professors of Medicine Francesco Bonafede and Pietro da Noale, and their students, with the aim of cultivating native and exotic medicinal plants for education and research. Many important people supported the initiative, for varying reasons. Politicians in the Venetian Senate, who took the decision to found the garden on 31 July, 1545, thought that the University would gain prestige from a medicinal garden enabling practical teaching. Merchants wanted to increase their profits from trading in exotic plants. The most important supporters were the doctors and pharmacists, who were eager to establish reliable plant identification and learn more about the therapeutic properties of different plants. The name of the person who designed the garden is not recorded, but nobleman Daniele Barbaro was certainly involved in the project and so was the architect Andrea Moroni of Bergamo.

Seeds and plants arrived at the great port of Venice, east of Padua, from Constantinople, Syria and Egypt, and as the collection was gradually extended it came to include plants from more far-flung places, such as the Americas. The Orto Botanico played an important role in the introduction to Europe of exotic plants, such as lilac (*Syringa vulgaris*, 1565), yellow jasmine (*Jasminum fruticans*, 1590), the edible sunflower (*Helianthus annuus*, 1568) and the potato (*Solanum tuberosum*, 1590). The plants were carefully studied by scientists who were looking mainly for species with therapeutic powers, which on their own or mixed with others could become medicines. By August

Above
Left The circular garden created in 1545, seen from the second floor of the University building. Intersected by two paths, the garden is divided into four quarters, like a medieval cloister garden, with a small fountain in the middle. The different species are planted according to their continent of origin and native climate.
Right A pond with water lilies.

1834 there were some 6,000 plants in the garden, but after the violent storms that occurred on one fateful day that month only half that number remained.

The garden was an instant success, attracting scientists from all over the world. Some were inspired to create botanical gardens in their home countries, for example at Leiden in the Netherlands, Heidelberg in Germany and Krakow in Poland. The Padua garden also became so popular among ordinary people that ten years after opening a wall had to be built to stop theft. But tomatoes and potatoes were left untouched – newly arrived in Europe, they were viewed with suspicion and no one dared eat them.

Astonishingly, the circular garden looks almost the same today as it did 450 years ago. The garden is surrounded by a circular enclosing wall and a meandering canal. Inside are some hundred small plots of land laid out in beautiful but simple geometrical patterns. Criss-crossed by paths leading to the points of the compass, the circular area is divided into four quadrangles and eight triangles. The design is inspired by medieval gardens: the circle, noblest of shapes, was considered divine during the Middle Ages and the Renaissance; the central fountain symbolizes the Well of Life; and the four squares represent the four continents then known: Europe, Africa, Asia and America.

The garden was enriched with plants from all over the world. Just inside the garden's outer wall are two giant magnolias (*Magnolia grandiflora*) from the southern United States, planted in the nineteenth century. The garden also contains Europe's oldest surviving magnolia, planted about 1700. If you follow the paths, you will soon reach the gates representing the four main compass points.

Opposite
Left The orchids grow hanging from tree branches in a shady area of the park. They are more likely to survive if they are allowed to grow in a natural way.
Top right The most poisonous plant in the garden is the castor oil plant (*Ricinus communis*), with its deceptively attractive bronze-coloured leaves.
Middle right In small ponds, similar to planting squares, the aquatic plants thrive. The giant water lily *Victoria cruziana* lives in a pool fed by an underground spring that keeps a constant temperature of 25°C (77°F).
Bottom right The plants came from all over the world to the port of Venice before finding their way to Orto Botanico in Padua. This sacred lotus flower (*Nelumbo nucifera*) originates in India.

Other landmarks include the hexagonal greenhouse, which contains one of the oldest plants in the garden. This is a palm tree (*Chamaerops humilis* var. *arborescens*), planted in 1585, which so fascinated Goethe during a visit here that he wrote about it in an essay on the metamorphosis of plants. Until the 1980s, the oldest plant in the garden was a chaste tree (*Vitex agnus-castus*) from the sixteenth century. It was about 450 years old when it died of a fungal disease.

Elsa Cappelletti, Professor in Padua's Department of Biology and Prefect of the garden from 1994 to 2000 and again from 2003, shows me around. She clearly inherited her interest in botany from her father Carlo Cappelletti, who was head of the department from 1948 to 1970.

The garden is laid out in an educational way. There is an area for carnivorous plants: for example, the Venus fly trap (*Dionaea muscipula*), which snares insects by closing its midrib; sundews, which have lots of glandular hairs and secrete sticky mucilage to attract and catch insects passively; and the pitcher plant (*Sarracenia* sp.), whose leaves form a vessel shape in which insects are caught and then dissolved by the plant's enzymes. There is a separate part of the garden for medicinal plants, and one for poisonous plants. Below the palm house, aquatic plants share small water-filled basins, and a tree in the shade is full of what look like cut-off tree trunks hanging upside down; here orchids grow in a strange but, for them, natural way.

Many of Padua's imported plants spread throughout Europe during the following centuries. Had this not happened, maybe we would not have the natural sources of some of today's effective medicines, or be able to enjoy the aroma of freshly made coffee or a wonderfully fragrant rose. Thank you, Orto Botanico! Perhaps the seven rules carved in stone by the entrance have helped to keep the garden in good condition:

Please don't walk in the garden before 25th April.
If you come in anyway, please stick to the paths.
Please don't pick any flowers.
Please don't step on any low-growing plants.
Please don't damage any plants.
Please don't do anything against the will of the Prefect!
QUI SECUS FAXIT AERE CARCERE EXSILIO MULTATOR.*

*If you break these rules, you will be fined, imprisoned and exiled!

Victoria
cruziana Orb
Bolivia-Paraguay

PROFUSION OF FLOWERS BY LAKE GARDA
ORIGINAL GARDEN DESIGNED BY VINCENZO PELLESINA FROM 1617
CURRENT LAYOUT BY ENZO SIGURTÀ TWENTIETH CENTURY

Parco Sigurtà

Valeggio sul Mincio

At the southern end of Lake Garda, not far from the beautiful city of Verona, is the enormous Sigurtà landscape garden. The house and a walled garden were created in 1617 by Vincenzo Pellesina, who was a pupil of Andrea Palladio (see page 152). The villa was originally called Maffei, and in 1859 it was used for a while by Emperor Napoleon III as his headquarters. The main work of transforming the arid hillside into a verdant park was started by owner Carlo Sigurtà and continued by his grandson Enzo Sigurtà in the twentieth century.

Today most of the well-kept garden is open to visitors; only a small part remains private. Covering a large area, it has some 30,000 plants and trees in flower from March until November. Among the many different garden areas are wonderfully lush green lawns, which are often full of people picnicking. You can get around by walking, hiring a golf cart, riding a bike or even by taking a ride on the miniature train that runs for four miles along the Magic Route. The trip takes you past several garden rooms with box trees cut into surreal shapes, ponds containing tropical fish, a herb garden, a rose walk and open green lawns with pine trees and Japanese maples.

Left
Top The large lawns of Parco Sigurtà are perfect for picnics and for enjoying the open air with friends and family. The statue is of Enzo Sigurtà, who created the layout of the park as we see it today.
Bottom A collection of exotic maples in beautifully contrasting colours.

INSPIRED BY THE STRIFE OF LOVE IN A DREAM

DESIGNED BY LUIGI TREZZA FOR ANTONIO RIZZARDI FROM 1783

Villa Rizzardi

Pojega di Negrar

In 1783, Count Antonio Rizzardi commissioned the architect Luigi Trezza to design and create a traditional Italian garden. Rizzardi's vision was of a garden with secret rooms, like those described by the monk Francesco Colonna in his allegorical text *Hypnerotomachia Poliphili* (1499). The park-like garden, in the midst of vineyards, is ambitious and made up of many lush, themed garden rooms, of which the Green Theatre is the most famous, with its rows of seats surrounded by clipped box and statues of actors in hornbeam niches. There is also an oval room, crowned by a *laghetto* (pond) surrounded by laurels and cypresses; and in the middle of a *boschetto* (small wood) is a temple-like building covered in artificial stalactites. From the first floor of the house, a bridge leads to the *giardino segreto* on the hill behind. Wherever you turn there are wonderful vistas; an avenue of elegant, precisely pruned cypresses, for example, leads to the house from the Green Theatre. The formal garden nearest the building displays modern bronze statues, which make an interesting contrast to the topiary and the historic setting. The sculptures are by Spanish artist Miguel Berrocal, who rents the villa as a home and studio.

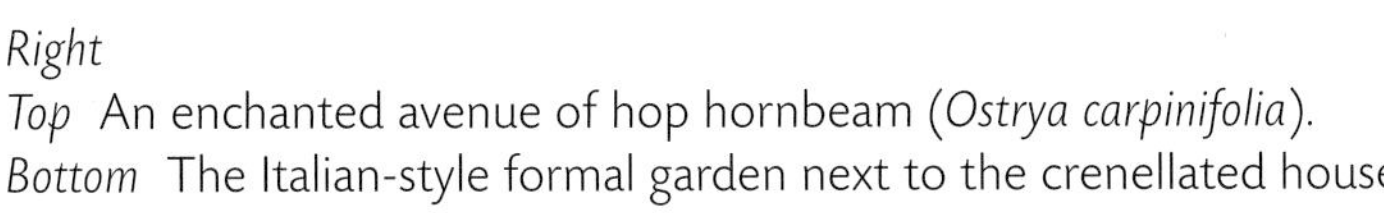

Right
Top An enchanted avenue of hop hornbeam (*Ostrya carpinifolia*).
Bottom The Italian-style formal garden next to the crenellated house.

A VILLA FOR WORK AND PLEASURE

Designed by Andrea Palladio for Daniele Barbaro 1550s

Villa Barbaro

Maser

Opposite Villa Barbaro represents the best of two worlds – that of the gentleman and that of the farmer – with a central building providing living quarters and two wings where harvested crops and farming equipment could be kept. The rooms are decorated with sixteenth-century paintings by Paolo Veronese showing contemporary country life.

Andrea Palladio (1508–80) is one of Italy's most important architects. His ideas about proportion, and about the relationship between architecture and the surrounding landscape, remain valid and continue to influence architecture and garden design. The same is even true of his theories of water recycling, put into practice at Villa Barbaro.

Nearly all Palladio's country estates in north-eastern Italy are situated high up in the rolling hills of the Venetian landscape. Taking as his starting point the buildings of Antiquity, Palladio planned his villas – including buildings, gardens and surrounding farmland – as integrated units with space for all activities, both work and pleasure. He would set aside land for a beautiful garden around the building, which would have a simple façade but be richly decorated inside. In the arcaded wings, there would be plenty of room for animals and farming equipment. A Palladian villa is often a working farm, but with plenty of space for relaxation and enjoyment.

Palladio's strengths lay not just in his sense of proportion and architectural harmony but also in his practical engineering skills. He employed these imaginatively to make the most efficient use of resources. His ideas can be found in his book *I Quattro Libri dell'Architettura* (1570), in which he describes, for example, the use of water at Villa Barbaro: 'The water comes from a fountain at the back of the house; it forms a small lake, which is used as a fishpond, and from there it flows into the kitchen. It then irrigates the gardens on either side of the road which slowly ascends to the house, and finally forms two ponds with accompanying water troughs next to the public road. It continues to irrigate the park, which is very large and full of splendid fruit trees and diverse wildlife.' This is recycling of the highest order!

Palladio was also involved in the first Italian translation of *De Architectura* (1556), the most important textual source concerning Roman architecture, written by Vitruvius in

the first century BC. Palladio contributed the drawings, and the translation and commentary were provided by Daniele Barbaro, the owner of Villa Barbaro. Daniele Barbaro was one of the intellectual patrons of the Renaissance, who, together with the Medicis and the Trissino family, showed everyone how to enjoy the country life. He was also one of the initiators of the Orto Botanico in Padua (see page 146).

In contrast with other villas of the time, the exteriors of and the ideas behind Palladio's buildings and gardens make them seem very modern. It is hard to believe that, for example, Pirro Ligorio's Villa d'Este near Rome (see page 34) was created at around the same time as Palladio's Villa Barbaro in Maser. Whereas Villa d'Este sits right in the middle of the village of Tivoli, and is separated from the open landscape of fields and olive groves by a wall, Palladio's Villa Barbaro blends in with the landscape, the border between the estate and the surrounding fields being undefined.

The only part of Palladio's magnificent garden layout to survive today is the *giardino segreto* behind the house. In her book *Italian Gardens*, Georgina Masson describes it as follows: 'In a small space – it is entirely enclosed by the house and hillside – it contrives to give an extraordinary feeling of grandeur, unequalled and not even approached by other gardens in the area. The whole effect is achieved by the semicircular fountain with its "infinity of *stucchi*", whose richness is offset by the dark green of the wooded hillside and the clear waters of the pool that lies in front.'

The twenty Palladian villas that still exist continue to inspire architects across the world: his style has been imitated in thousands of buildings, mainly in the United States and Britain. One of the most famous outside Italy is the Villa Monticello in Virginia, once the home of President Thomas Jefferson.

MODERN STYLE IN A HISTORIC SETTING

DESIGNED BY CARLO SCARPA FROM 1949

Above A concrete wall inlaid with gold and silver tiles. Below is a bronze basin filled with the fallen petals of a cherry tree.

Opposite A water channel in terrazzo. The exquisite details were designed by architect Carlo Scarpa and cast in bronze.

Palazzo Querini Stampalia

Venice

The beautiful façades of Venice seldom hide flowering courtyards or gardens that are open to the public. One exception is the art museum of the Fondazione Querini Stampalia. Found in the same piazza as Santa Maria Formosa, one of the oldest churches in the city, the museum is a Renaissance palace with a modern arch that spans the canal and leads into the building. The ground floor and the inner courtyard have been designed and restored by Carlo Scarpa, one of the most talented and poetic Italian architects of the twentieth century. He was commissioned in 1949 by the museum's then curator Manlio Dazzi to restore the courtyard and the garden, and he redesigned the ground floor ten years later.

It only takes a couple of minutes to wander around the tiny, charming garden. There is a long wall, completely covered in ivy. Opposite is a water channel cast in terrazzo. A closer look at details such as the bronze spout and the beautiful circular basin underneath reveals that Scarpa took great care in the restoration. The materials used for the decoration of the garden are simple – concrete, terrazzo and mosaic – but there is also bronze and some marble in the form of scattered Roman remains. At the other end of the terrazzo water channel I see a white bird in a birdbath. The bird has no idea that its bath is actually a work of art, in the shape of a labyrinth made of alabaster and Istrian stone.

On the lawn a spring-flowering cherry tree is in bloom; its pink petals have fallen into a square bronze basin. There are also magnolias, pomegranates and various climbers. When Venice's canals flood, as they do sometimes, a sophisticated system under the garden stops the courtyard from flooding. Carlo Scarpa has clearly shown that it is possible to combine a modern garden with a historic Renaissance building, provided that everything is done with the greatest care.

LIGURIA

THE WHOLE WORLD IN ONE PLACE
CREATED BY THE HANBURY FAMILY FROM 1867

Villa Hanbury
La Mortola

Pages 156–7 The steep hills of the glittering Ligurian coastline close to the French border are home to the exotic gardens of Villa Hanbury.

Above A bust of Sir Thomas stands in the loggia at Villa Hanbury. The view through the arches extends down to the coast near Ventimiglia.

Opposite, clockwise from top left A flowering crassula from South Africa (*Crassula perfoliata* var. *minor*); a Japanese sago palm (*Cycas revoluta*); a golden barrel cactus (*Echinocactus grusonii*), also known as mother-in-law's cushion, from Mexico; an agave (*Doryanthes palmeri*) from Australia.

It is the year 1867 and 35-year-old English businessman Thomas Hanbury is on holiday on the Côte d'Azur. During a boat trip on the Bay of Ventimiglia, close to the French border, he glimpses a beautiful south-facing promontory, a slope covered in olive groves, vineyards and cypresses that overlooks the glittering Mediterranean Sea.

The site was exactly what he had been looking for. Thomas Hanbury's aim was to develop the sort of experimental garden that was not possible in his native climate: he wanted to gather the plants of the world together and enjoy their flowers all year round. His participation in the Shanghai tea and silk trade had made him very rich, and had given him many contacts abroad. Together with his brother Daniel, who was a botanist and pharmacologist, he began to import seeds from all over the world. In 1889 he published *Hortus mortolensis*, his first catalogue of plants grown in the garden; it included 100 types of cactus alone.

Near the entrance at the top of the garden is a Chinese symbol carved in a stone; it means 'happiness' and was a gift from a friend in China. For Sir Thomas the establishment of Villa Hanbury was a dream come true. The promontory was to become home to one of the greatest collections of rare exotic plants in the world. He became well respected in the area, creating many jobs locally as well as undertaking other positive initiatives such as financing schools. When he died in 1907 a procession of 6,000 people attended the funeral.

After Thomas Hanbury's death the garden was developed by Lady Dorothy, the wife of his son Cecil. She laid out footpaths, created viewpoints and integrated fountains with the planting. Cecil and Dorothy also built the Giardinetti, a small traditional Italian garden next to the house. They introduced new plant varieties and began an extensive exchange of plants with the Royal Botanic Gardens at Kew.

Opposite In the foreground are flowering agaves. Villa Hanbury brings together plants from all over the world.

From the entrance, the footpath meanders down the hill in two branches. The drought-tolerant plants can be found in the upper parts of the garden: cactuses (which in April display brilliantly coloured flowers) and succulents are gathered in decorative groups, and the aloes with their long, strong, silvery-grey leaves create a pleasing foreground to the view of the garden below. The small Four Seasons Temple, crowned with an ornamental iron cupola, is halfway down the garden, towards the house. Next to it, an agave sends up impressive stalks of yellow flowers that are reminiscent of burdock, but with bloomspikes facing upwards. Their silhouettes are striking against the blue sky. The Spanish dagger (*Yucca gloriosa*), which I've previously seen only as an indoor foliage plant, shows off upright sprays of white flowers, each one a pretty anemone-like bell.

Several sources mention Hanbury's plants. Every January, Sir Thomas wrote a column for the English magazine *Gardeners' Chronicle*, in which he would give an account of the plants flowering at the time. In January 1882, there were some 233 plants in bloom.

Behind the Fountain of the Dragon – an angry dragon balancing on the edge of a basin – is a wall of papyrus with delicate plumes. The garden also contains some more traditional Mediterranean plants, like the white and purple wisteria, and the acacia trees that give off a wonderful scent early in the year. Angel's trumpets, orange trees, spiraeas in long borders and Judas trees (*Cercis siliquastrum*) can be found along the paths.

When you reach the house, there is still the other half of the garden left to see. If you continue down the slope, you will experience a different side of Villa Hanbury: next to the house is an Italian garden with formal straight hedges and flowering peonies. There are also meadows that are full of flowers in spring, while ivy climbs up the knotty trunks of an avenue of olive trees – just before you reach a simple, but much longed-for café. Unfortunately, from here the sea is hidden behind the house and a wall.

In 1960 Lady Dorothy sold the gardens to the Italian government, and since 1998 Villa Hanbury has been run by the University of Genoa. Recreating and restoring the garden according to Thomas Hanbury's original plan has been a long and expensive process. The exchange of seeds with other botanical gardens still goes on; to avoid hybridization it's important to collect seeds from their original habitat and the office lists 600 gardens with which Villa Hanbury has contact. There is also a continuing exchange of knowledge, through a scheme that gives students of horticulture an opportunity to live and work in the garden while they are undertaking research.

A GARDEN IN THREE ACTS

DESIGNED BY MICHELE CANZIO 1840

Villa Durazzo

Pegli-Genoa

Originally know as Villa Grimaldi, Villa Durazzo was created in 1840 by Michele Canzio, an architect and stage designer from Genoa. This romantic landscape park is an amalgamation of an eighteenth-century botanic garden and the garden of a palazzo. The park also contains an archaeological museum.

Walking through the garden is a unique experience thanks to the variety of the settings and the plantings. Canzio's idea was to make the visitor feel like the hero or heroine of a fairy tale, passing through the garden as if through a theatrical drama with a prologue and three acts.

During the walk, the visitor is supposed to reflect on the meaning of life as it is expressed in the changing surroundings. Leaving a classic boulevard with an elegant fountain in the middle, you suddenly find yourself in an Alpine landscape. A short stroll later and you are surrounded by an oasis of Mediterranean plants, before reaching an avenue of camellias. There are small buildings scattered around the park, each with its own identity: a coffee house pavilion, the retreat known as the Hermit's House and a Swiss cabin. As you leave the gloom of the artificial grottoes, you step into the bright surroundings of a large lake that represents spiritual fulfilment. In the lake is a Temple of Diana; there is also a Roman bridge, a Turkish kiosk, a Chinese pagoda and an Egyptian obelisk. Finally, you reach an earthly paradise in the form of a garden of Flora. Everything in the park has its own meaning – although today the symbolic codes can be hard to crack.

Left
Top The Temple of Diana, in a lake that represents the attainment of spiritual paradise.
Middle The shadows give way as you emerge from the caves into light by the lake.
Bottom A great variety of palms grow in the botanical garden of Villa Durazzo.

HANGING FROM A CLIFF TOP

CREATED BY MARQUIS DURAZZO
FROM 1868

ey of La Cervara

Ligure

m to have a knack for finding the loveliest settings for their f the most beautifully situated abbeys in Italy, perched high on a Gerolamo della Cervara. While the abbey was first built for the ks in 1361, it was not until 1868 that Marquis Durazzo created, on a king the sea, the main garden as we see it today.

ance-style Italian garden is laid out on flat ground with box parterres netrical patterns. There are also imaginative topiary hemispheres of box, h decorative swirling bands. In the centre is a fountain with a stone cherub. nks the edge of the terrace and leads on to the Wisteria Courtyard, which n 500-year-old blue wisteria with impressive stems and branches.

ath the Portofino Terrace, at the other end of the garden, there was once a l. Here the French king Francis I was held for a while in 1525, after being at Pavia by the Holy Roman Emperor, Charles V. His time in prison is not likely een a pleasant experience, but he would at least have had a nice sea view from indow, with the coastline of the village of Portofino just visible to the south.

lower terrace of the garden's two levels is beautifully and imaginatively laid out, with box forming geometrical patterns and topiary box cones flanking the central path.

LOMBARDY & P

The Abb

Santa Margherita

Monks and nuns see
monasteries. One c
headland, is San
Benedictine mor
terrace overloo

The Renaiss
forming geor
crowned wi
A loggia fla
is covered i

Underne
prison cel
defeated
to have b
his cell w

Above Th
hedges of

EDMONT

DIVINE VIEWS FROM A PROMONTORY
ORIGINAL LAYOUT CREATED FOR ANGELO MARIA DURINI 1790
REDESIGNED BY EMILIO TRABELLA FOR GUIDO MONZINO 1970S

Villa Balbianello

Lenno

It is early morning when, full of expectations, I open the French windows of my hotel room to look out across the dark blue waters of Lake Como. But my eyes come to rest on the balustrade – beyond it is thick, steely-grey fog. I take a deep breath of the fresh, oxygen-rich air, before going down to the quayside to wait for the taxi boat.

We leave at seven o'clock, just as the contours of the shore are becoming visible. The journey is refreshing and the fog gradually thins into milky-white veils of mist. In the distance I can see, more and more clearly, the promontory of Dosso di Lavedo, as well as the church that balances on its tip. We will soon reach what in my opinion is the most beautiful setting of any of the gardens in northern Italy. Near the two church spires, plane trees create intricate patterns in the air. We finally arrive at the landing place, which is flanked by four Venetian red-and-white-striped poles.

Villa Balbianello is not a colourful flowering garden; the planting has been deliberately designed around shades of green. The striking elements are the plane trees, the pruning and, of course, the setting. What really makes the garden special is its location. Right out on the tip of the promontory, the garden is surrounded by sheer drops on three sides. The vistas are stunning: to the south is the island of Comacina, set off against the sunlight; to the north is a deep lake against a backdrop of snow-capped mountains.

From the small quay, a path sweeps elegantly uphill through a curved avenue of plane trees. In summer, the trees protect against the hot sun; the viewpoint in front of the church will be cool and the avenue will provide a shaded walk with divine views in every direction.

Pages 164–5 The deep blue waters of Lake Como meet the sky and the snow-covered Alps in the lake district of northern Italy. Villa Balbianello is just visible on a promontory in the distance.

Opposite The knotty, sculptural latticework of the branches of the plane trees (*Platanus acerifolia*) creates wreaths against the blue sky. In April the trees are still bare, but they will soon have the lush crowns of leaves that provide shade during the hot summers.

Opposite, clockwise from top left: A view from the boat of Villa Balbianello on the promontory Dosso di Lavedo, with the village of Lenno in the background; the view from the north terrace, framed by an elegant balustrade; holm oak (*Quercus ilex*) closely pruned to ensure the view of the house is not obstructed; plane trees (*Platanus acerifolia*) wearing what might be described as ivy 'leg warmers'.

All the plants and trees have been pruned with the greatest of precision. 'The garden needs constant maintenance all year round. Its beauty lies in the interplay of views and perspective, which would be lost if the plants were not constantly pruned,' says landscape architect Emilio Trabella, who started to work for the owner, Guido Monzino, in the 1970s. When you see their strictly pruned shapes, you sometimes have to remind yourself that the ivy, guelder rose, laurel, jasmine and wintercreeper in this garden are actually living plants.

During the steep walk I notice that ivy has been trained around the trunks of the plane trees in an unusual and imaginative way. On the left-hand side of the path, a dextrous gardener has created garlands of ivy on a low stone wall. Opposite, draped over iron railings, are racemes of wisteria that have just burst into flower. The gardener has allowed daisies to remain in the grass on the slope, which is a nice touch in this otherwise perfect garden.

And what would an Italian garden be without cypresses? At Villa Balbianello the cypresses are perfectly formed, like spears or living obelisks. There are also firs and pines, and camphor trees, agaves and holm oaks. Near the wooded part of the promontory, the caretaker's rural cottage can be found, behind a lush group of flowering azaleas. They brighten up the garden, their red colour a striking contrast to the evergreen plants.

It was Franciscan monks who discovered the soul of the place, in the thirteenth century. The promontory is surrounded by water, mountains and sky, and must have been the perfect place for a simple spiritual and reflective life. Having passed through the hands of several owners within the Church, the estate was bought in 1787 by Cardinal Angelo Maria Durini, who created the overall look of today's Villa Balbianello. The oratory, convent and two bell towers already existed; he added a casino at the top of the hill and a gracious linking loggia with three arcades. Wintercreepers (*Euonymus radicans*) now climb vigorously over the loggia, creating beautiful garlands.

The terrain at Villa Balbianello was not suitable for a formal garden; it would have been very difficult to plant a knot garden with box hedges across the slopes. But some features of the formal style can be found. Between the plane trees are statues of mythological figures gazing out across the lake, amongst them the fertility goddess Flora with a basket of flowers and the wine god Bacchus covered in grapes. In the garden there are remains from Antiquity, as well as art bought as late as the 1970s.

The American General Butler Ames, his wife Fifi and their heirs owned the villa between 1919 and 1974. She loved fuchsias and was known as Signora della Fuchsia. As Emilio Trabella explains, they left behind a richly flowering garden: 'At that time the garden looked very different and there was no consistency, probably due to a custom of the owner. Before leaving, guests were asked to buy a plant of their own choice, which would be put in the garden with a card showing their name and the date of their visit.'

Count Guido Monzino bought the villa in 1974. After an exciting life as a businessman and later as an explorer (there was an expedition to the North Pole in 1971 and another to Mount Everest in 1973), Guido Monzino was looking for a new challenge. Together with landscape architect Emilio Trabella, he transformed the garden with great enthusiasm and skill. The overall design remained true to the eighteenth-century layout introduced by Cardinal Durini, but details were changed to give a more modern impression: for example, evergreen trees such as box and laurel were shaped in an elegant and innovative way, in order to refine and simplify the garden.

Emilio Trabella explains what they discussed: 'Simplicity is the key word for understanding our work, a simplicity that recalls the original use of the villa as a hospital and the fact that even when it was turned into a noble residence it was never conceived as sumptuous. It has the simplicity of an English garden where the lawns are substituted by the lake that touches the promontory on three sides.'

One of Guido Monzino's projects was to create an uninterrupted view from his study to the north. He therefore decided to prune the giant holm oak (*Quercus ilex*) on the north terrace so that only the outer layer of the foliage remained. According to Emilio Trabello the pruning of the crown is still done with great care in order not to ruin the tree: the gardeners climb up into the crown, and once there cut everything that is 'higher than their belt'.

Count Monzino bequeathed the villa to the Fondo per l'Ambiente Italiano (FAI) in 1988. This was fortunate for us, as FAI maintains the estate and keeps it open to the public. Guido Monzino's tomb is in the garden, in a beautiful spot on the way down to the north terrace.

As I leave, I'm already beginning to miss the place. When will I be able to come back and experience again the wonderful atmosphere of this garden? Very soon, I hope.

GIANT RHODODENDRONS AND AZALEAS
BAROQUE GARDEN CREATED FOR GIORGIO CLERICI FROM 1745
LANDSCAPE GARDENS CREATED FOR GIOVANNI BATTISTA SOMMARIVA
AND CHARLOTTE AND GEORGE SAXE-MEININGEN IN THE NINETEENTH CENTURY

Villa Carlotta

Cadenabbia

The series of five terraces, seen from the house. The lowest of the fountains, depicting Arion being saved by a dolphin, is surrounded by clipped hedges of cherry laurel (*Prunus laurocerasus*), bay laurel (*Laurus nobilis*) and camellias (*Camellia japonica*).

A scenic but treacherously narrow road winds its way through the tiny strip of land between Lake Como and the mountains. This is the Via Regina, built by the Romans in the second century BC as a military route to the rest of Europe. On this road can be found the Villa Carlotta, which is the most interesting and the most famous of all the many beautiful villas along the lake. The garden blends Baroque architecture, romantic flowers and the English landscape style.

The entrance to Villa Carlotta is a short walk from the small boat landing in Cadenabbia, to the north of Tremezzo. The intricately ornate iron gate is decorated with a big letter C to commemorate the Clerici family, who built the villa during the seventeenth and eighteenth centuries. The villa was designed in a style known as Lombard High Baroque, by an architect whose name has not survived.

The head of the family was Marquis Giorgio Clerici, a Milanese banker and President of the Lombardian Senate. He transformed the sloping bank of the lake into a series of terraces conforming to the principles of formal garden design, in which geometry and regularity are the most important characteristics. The front part of the garden at Villa Carlotta is laid out around a main axis that divides stairs, balustrades and terraces into two symmetrical parts. From the gate, the garden rises steeply between twin staircases to the entrance to the house, where the imaginary bisecting line continues, inside through the atrium and then out again into the rear courtyard. I stand at the bottom of the garden, looking up towards the house, and try to get a feel for the 'balance of harmony' – and yes, it is there. But the sensation isn't entirely positive: I feel so small compared to the large scale and long perspectives used in the design. The building speaks of power and influence – which, of course, is exactly what it was meant to do.

The scent of oranges and lemons overwhelms me. On both sides of the staircase citrus trees climb up pergolas; they were virtually all that was planted during the first hundred years of the garden's history. To the left are beautiful, but perhaps too harshly pruned camellia hedges. Dappled sunlight dances across soft pink petals that have fallen to the ground. Further to the left is the oldest part of the park, where the Cascades of the Pygmies, an unusual creation of fountains and grottoes, can be found.

At the end of the eighteenth century, Giovanni Battista Sommariva of Milan took over the estate and began to develop it. At the same time, his neighbour across the lake in Bellagio, Chancellor Francesco Melzi, was busy augmenting his own house and garden (see page 176). Both men were very rich and tried to outdo each other in the creation of a magnificent estate.

Marianne of Prussia purchased the villa in 1843 and later gave it as a wedding present to her daughter Charlotte. The estate became known as Villa Carlotta. Charlotte and her husband, Prince George of Saxe-Meiningen, adapted the formal Italian style by creating a picturesque garden that, with its glades, meandering pathways and viewing points, seemed to be more in tune with the surrounding landscape. Exotic and rare plants were imported from all over the world, adding species to the collection of azaleas and rhododendrons that Sommariva had started.

More than a hundred different types of azalea and rhododendron grow here, and they are all skilfully pruned. They were imported from Asia during the nineteenth century, when it was fashionable among Europeans to take an interest in that continent. The flowers are shocking pink, purple, lilac and white, and their intense colours form a beautiful pattern like an Oriental carpet. A courting couple strolls past the azaleas hand in hand, and it suddenly dawns on me how enormously tall these plants are – some are almost 10 metres (30 feet) high.

A botanical paradise. The flowering of azaleas and rhododendrons is at its peak in the last week of April. When they have finished flowering in June, there are still more than 600 species of plants and trees to discover in the seventeen acres of the garden. Among them are ninety types of camellia, twenty-two types of bamboo and thirty-eight types of rose, according to the plant list. Behind the rock garden, a thriving Chinese wisteria (*Wisteria sinensis*) is busy climbing up into the crown of an Austrian pine (*Pinus nigra*). To the left, a gigantic blue Atlas cedar (*Cedrus atlantica* 'Glauca') spreads its silvery-green branches.

Opposite, clockwise from top left: Villa Carlotta from the lake; some of the azaleas of every conceivable colour and shape that blanket the garden; demure forget-me-nots and red tulips on one of the terraces, with the Sommariva Oratory in the background to the left; a meandering path, flanked by tall azaleas, that guides the visitor through the garden.

Opposite Villa Carlotta is known not just for azaleas, but also for its camellias. Here, in the wooded area of the garden, is a path surrounded by camellias in bloom.

Having passed through the collections of succulents, cacti and palm trees, I cross a bridge over a mountain stream and enter a totally different climate. A tulip tree (*Liriodendron tulipifera*) with perfectly shaped, rounded leaves creates a roof of branches above me, its lush yellow-green flowers brightening up the dark ravine. The stream is surrounded by Australian tree ferns (*Alsophila australis*, also known as *Cyathea*) and smooth tree ferns (*Dicksonia antarctica*). It is very humid here and the lush greenery makes the place seem wild, like an unexplored forest. But the truth is that many of these plants are so sensitive that they are put in glasshouses during the cold winter months and then placed outside again in spring.

Further into the garden are several beautiful and exotic trees, among them a group of southern magnolias (*Magnolia grandiflora*), with their shiny leathery leaves. Two species of camphor tree are also found here, *Cinnamomum camphora* as well as *C. glanduliferum*, whose leaves when crushed give off a fine scent. By the picnic area is a dawn redwood (*Metasequoia glyptostroboides*), a weeping rosebud cherry (*Prunus subhirtella miq.* 'Pendula rubra') and a *P. lusitanica*.

The bamboo garden is 200 metres (650 feet) above sea level. After passing through a *torii*, a Japanese gate made from larch wood, I enter bamboo heaven. Here dwarf bamboo is mixed with many different species of larger bamboo, such as the gigantic *Phyllostachys edulis* 'Bicolor' and *P. pubescens* var. *heterocycla* 'Kikkochiku'.

I decide to take a look at the art collection in the house, in particular at Francesco Hayez's 1823 oil painting *The Last Kiss of Romeo and Juliet*, inspired by William Shakespeare's drama. Many other famous artists, amongst them the sculptor Antonio Canova, have also left their mark in the form of painted ceilings, paintings and statues. Fascinated, I stop in the Statue Room for a closer look at the Danish sculptor Bertel Thorvaldsen's 1812 marble frieze, *Alexander the Great's Triumphal Entry into Babylon*.

During the First World War, the villa was confiscated by the Italian government. The estate was to be used as a nursing home for war veterans, but instead it became a museum and garden open to the public. The garden is the perfect product of the talents of three families: the Clericis, who found the unique setting and laid out the Baroque garden; Sommariva, the art lover who created the framework for a romantic landscape garden; and finally the Saxe-Meiningens, who added a third dimension – the garden as a botanical paradise.

ROMANCE BY LAKE COMO

DESIGNED BY CANONICA AND VILLORESI FOR FRANCESCO MELZI D'ERIL 1808–10

Above View of Villa Melzi in Bellagio. In the neoclassical style, the house is surrounded by a romantic landscape garden with meandering paths and spectacular vistas.

Opposite In summer, an avenue of plane trees (*Platanus acerifolia*) provides visitors with shade. The branches at the top of the trees are harshly pruned so that they don't interfere with the view across the lake.

Villa Melzi

Bellagio

It is late afternoon on the eastern shore of Lake Como, and the spectacular view from the top of the hill makes me stop by the roadside. Sharply silhouetted snow-tipped mountains rise up out of the lake; the scene is like a watercolour painted in blues, greys and milky whites. I am reminded of all those northern Europeans who travelled to Italy, full of dreams, during the eighteenth and nineteenth centuries. They must have been happy when they finally reached Lake Como, exhausted after the tough journey across the mountains. This was their very first view of the 'dream of Italy' – and they were surely not disappointed.

I'm on my way to Villa Melzi in the village of Bellagio, at the juncture of the two legs of the upside-down 'Y' that makes up the distinctive shape of Lake Como. Villa Melzi is just south of Bellagio, with entrances to its long garden from both Bellagio and Loppia. It was built for Chancellor Francesco Melzi d'Eril in 1808–10 to plans by the famous architect Giocondo Albertolli. In 1802 Melzi and his neighbour across the lake, Giovanni Battista Sommariva, had both been candidates for the Vice-Presidency of the newly formed Republic of Italy. The rivalry of the two men was expressed in their efforts to outdo each other in the creation of a ostentatious country estate (see page 171). Villa Melzi, which resembles a small palace, is certainly impressive. It is built in a typical neoclassical style, which at the time stood for freedom of expression and innovation, and represented a move away from the ornate Baroque styles of the past.

On a spring day at the end of March, Ludovico Melzi, direct descendant of the founder of Villa Melzi, is busy helping out in the garden. Dressed in a brown gaberdine suit and a pair of well-worn walking shoes, he's weeding in the area surrounding the Japanese Lake. Slightly out of breath, he tells me that it's hard to keep the garden looking perfect, as he's the only member of the family interested in spending time on

Opposite A little building near the edge of the water is reminiscent of a Turkish kiosk. This is where the composer Franz Liszt liked to sit when he visited Villa Melzi. In the foreground are flowering azaleas.

it. He is himself often busy with his work as a lawyer, and employs part-time gardeners. The Melzi family used to grow vines on the slopes above the lake, but the farm had to be closed down after the plants were hit by frost several years running, and the garden was opened to the public. Ludovico Melzi explains to me that growing vines is no longer profitable, but the garden's rare and exotic plants flourish thanks to a favourable microclimate.

During the nineteenth century, Lake Como was already a popular recreational destination. It was mainly the 'old families' who turned their grand villas into hotels for the aristocracy. Then the word reached politicians, actors and other famous people, who came here to breathe the fresh air and meet like-minded people. Fishing, once the main source of income for the area, was overtaken by tourism. On the shores of Lake Como the air was clear, the light breezes were refreshing and the close proximity to water had a cooling effect in the summer heat. Some visitors even took a dip in the water – a fashion which had spread across Europe from the south coast of England, where doctors recommended sea bathing as a cure for a range of ailments.

Next to the house a romantic landscape garden extends, with its meandering pathways and exotic trees and plants. One of only a handful of visitors, I wander around in the afternoon sun. The planting is beautiful, and the garden complements the house and the surrounding mountains and the lake superbly. Despite knowing that every square metre has been well thought out, I get the impression that the architects of the garden, Canonica and Villoresi, had the confidence to design with a light touch.

Villa Melzi was the first garden in the area in the so-called English style, and the work of landscaping must have demanded a lot of muscle power. Large amounts of soil had to be dug up and moved in order to create new vistas and to give the right illusionary perspectives, fooling the eye according to Classical ideals. Flat areas were turned into undulating hills, and stone-covered pathways were laid out on the rocks. The main axis, around which the garden is planned, extends from the lake to a point high up in the hills where meandering paths criss-cross, creating a charmingly natural scene. I take a seat on a bench and look out across the clear mountain lake, surrounded by mountain ranges. The view is set off by a copper beech (*Fagus sylvatica* 'Purpurea') and two shiny Chilean wine palms (*Jubaea chilensis*).

The slope down towards the water is covered by several thickets of tall azaleas, which were planted in the early twentieth century when exotic plants were being imported on

Around the Japanese Lake are many exotic trees, such as this Japanese maple (*Acer palmatum*) whose rusty-red crown is reflected in the dark water.

a large scale. During three to four weeks from the middle of April, the azaleas of Villa Melzi are swathed in cerise, pink and white flowers. This is the best time to visit the garden, preferably in late afternoon when the sunshine filters down through the trees.

By the lakeside is a small, white, octagonal building with a blue cupola. It looks rather exotic with its domed roof and rounded window frames. Is it a summerhouse, a Greek temple, a Chinese pagoda, a music pavilion or perhaps a Turkish kiosk? I look up the explanation of 'kiosk' in my reference book, and discover that the word refers to the sort of small, open, onion-domed building that was introduced to Europe in the eighteenth century as an Oriental feature in English gardens. So, a kiosk it is then!

One of many regular guests at Villa Melzi was the composer Franz Liszt, who spent a number of seasons in Bellagio. So too did the French writer Stendhal (whose real name was Henri Beyle). Liszt would compose music as he sat in the kiosk by the water; maybe he was inspired by the nearby sculpture of Dante and Beatrice when he wrote his famous *Dante Sonata*. During the nineteenth century, theatre and drama were in vogue, and as a result the planning of Villa Melzi's garden was at that time approached as a piece of drama. The garden was supposed to arouse different moods and feelings, of which the most important were held to be delight, surprise and fright!

Japanese maples (*Acer palmatum*) are reflected in the water by a little bridge, where I also find a coast redwood tree (*Sequoia sempervirens*). Further along is a camphor tree (*Cinnamomum camphora*) opposite two exotic pines, the Oriental *Pinus longifolia* and *P. montezumae* from Mexico. On the slope above the kiosk is a solid-looking tulip tree (*Liriodendron tulipifera*), with beautifully shaped leaves. A grand red oak (*Quercus rubra*) grows further up the hill, in the very middle of the garden.

I end my visit with a stroll through an avenue of plane trees (*Platanus acerifolia*) and gaze out across the still water, which resembles a silvery-blue silk carpet in the afternoon light. Many famous people have walked in the shade of these plane trees. One of the regular guests, who spent a lot of time at Villa Melzi, was Josephine, wife of Napoleon Bonaparte. Her husband was given much support from the Vice-President of the short-lived Republic of Italy, which lasted only from 1802 until 1805. The man in question was Chancellor Francesco Melzi d'Eril, the first owner and creator of Villa Melzi. The estate is still owned by the Melzi family today.

BOTANICAL MIRACLE CREATED BY A GLACIER
CREATED FOR THE BORROMEO FAMILY FROM 1501

Isola Madre

Lake Maggiore

Blue wisteria grows abundantly above a staircase leading to the lake. Lush vegetation covers most of Isola Madre.

Isola Madre, one of the Borromean Islands in Lake Maggiore, is a miracle of nature. Thanks to a temperate microclimate of humid summers and mild sunny winters, the 125 acres of Isola Madre provide a perfect growing environment in which plants from all over the world can thrive.

Immediately above the landing place, next to the ticket office, grows a beautiful Chinese mandarin tree (*Cunninghamia lanceolata*). And those who have been to the Himalayas may recognize the giant rhododendrons, the tallest of which is 15 metres (50 feet) high. Head gardener Gianfranco Giustina, himself 2 metres (6½ feet) tall, is dwarfed by these huge trees.

Gianfranco has worked in Isola Madre for over twenty years. He describes the island's creation and the consequences of the garden's unusual position in the middle of a lake. When the climate changed at the end of the last ice age, he explains, temperatures rose and the ice melted. Out of the enormous pressure of water and ice, Isola Madre was created. At the bottom of the lake, scientists have discovered a double S formation that shows how rocks were squashed together and upwards, until the island was pushed above the water. Isola Madre's favourable climate – not too hot, not too cold – comes from being surrounded by water. During summer, heat is stored in the waters of the lake. In winter this heat is given off, resulting in warmer temperatures. The water also reflects light when the sun is low, enabling plants to thrive during the winter months.

Attracted by the climate, Count Lancillotto Borromeo bought the island in 1501. A simple house was put up on the ruins of a Roman fort, and an orchard was planted alongside the ancient olive trees already growing on the island. Lancillotto brought over orange and lemon trees (which are uncommon this far north), mulberry trees and vines.

The geographer Leandro Alberti's book *Descrittione di tutta Italia* describes what grew on the island in 1550: '550 grapevines, 9 walnut trees, 4 fig trees, 8 olive trees,

Below top The rhododendron wood has many specimens more than 10 metres (30 feet) high. *Below bottom* A stunning display of tail feathers by a peacock in the garden of Isola Madre. *Opposite* A white peacock shows off its beauty in front of a copse of pink flowering azaleas. The white peacock has become a symbol of the Borromean Islands and of the town of Stresa.

2 chestnut trees, 2 cherry trees, 17 quince trees, 8 pomegranate trees, 6 apple trees and "other small plants".'

Lancillotto died in 1513, and the work was continued by Renato I Borromeo. In 1583 Renato commissioned the famous architect Pellegrino Tibaldi to rebuild the simple house as a Renaissance villa (the building he created is still owned by the Borromeo family). The plan of the garden was not drawn up until a couple of decades later, by Giovanni Angelo Crivelli – the man behind the original design of Isola Bella (see page 184). By the end of the nineteenth century, the garden had been given the Picturesque English style that we see today.

Isola Madre is a landscape garden with exotic plants. Gianfranco Giustina shows me the Africa Avenue, which is the first part you reach when you arrive and the most sheltered and sunniest area of the garden. It is followed by the Terrace of the Camellias where the fragile plants have been growing since 1830, cared for by the mild winds. Banana plants, rhododendrons, ten types of wisteria, magnolias, hibiscuses, azaleas and laburnums also grow in the garden, along with the pampas grass (*Gynerium argenteum*), which in September has tall silvery plumes. If you're interested in palm trees you should find your way to the Palm Avenue, where you can admire a 125-year-old *Jubaea chilensis*.

There is a surprise around every corner. Secluded garden rooms turn into open areas. Shallow staircases lead away from the water and into a dense forest of rhododendrons. The variety of plants and trees is wonderful, contrasting with the more elegant austerity of Isola Bella. On the inner courtyard, in front of the palace's graceful loggia, stands a gigantic cypress that originates in the Himalayas. This spectacular *Cupressus cashmeriana* is the pride of the family; it is the largest in Europe, according to Gianfranco. On an open lawn, a white peahen is strutting about as if she owned the place. She's very beautiful – and she knows it.

Isola Madre is considered by many the most beautiful garden in Italy. Experts from abroad come here to study the plants, and Gianfranco himself travels widely in his quest for knowledge. He no longer buys plants, but instead swaps them with other botanical gardens all over the world.

THE FLOATING BAROQUE GARDEN

Designed by Giovanni Angelo Crivelli and Francesco Castelli for the Borromeo Family 1631–71

Above From a distance, Isola Bella resembles a gigantic Roman pleasure boat. The pyramid-shaped garden is laid out on ten terraces.

Opposite top On the lower terrace, the word *humilitas* has been created in flowers in honour of the sixteenth-century saint Carlo Borromeo, an ascetic dedicated to helping the sick and reforming the Church. His motto *humilitas* is used in the family coat of arms.

Opposite bottom The garden is richly adorned with statues including figures representing the four elements (air, earth, fire and water). Here Fire is personified as a strong man with an arrow in his left hand.

Isola Bella

Lake Maggiore

The best way to see Isola Bella is from a helicopter or a low-flying aeroplane. From the air you can clearly grasp the island's ship-like form, with ten terraces forming a flat-topped 'poop', and statues that might be sailors or passengers waving from the 'bridge'. The appearance is of a sixteenth-century galleon or perhaps an ancient pleasure craft. Maybe Count Carlo III Borromeo and his architect Giovanni Angelo Crivelli had been inspired by the two huge pleasure boats belonging to the first-century Roman Emperor Caligula, which were once kept anchored in Lake Nemi outside Rome. On board, as on Isola Bella, guests would have been entertained among the cool lake breezes during the hot days and nights of summer.

Isola Bella can be reached by boat from several villages around the lake. I catch a ferry from Pallanza and soon arrive at the tiny harbour in the village just below the Borromeo family's palace. To get to the garden, you must pass through the opulent Baroque palace, which is very impressive if rather too big for the size of the island. From an upstairs window, I can see a grassy lawn on which flowers grow in the pattern of the Borromeo coat of arms. From a bedroom facing southeast, the neighbouring island of Isola Madre is visible. Here the great conqueror Napoleon Bonaparte woke up one morning, after one of the triumphal battles that were to end in his victory at Venice on 12 May, 1797.

Carlo III Borromeo was Governor of the Lake Maggiore region. He inherited the Borromean Islands and named one of them Isola Isabella in honour of his wife, Isabella d'Adda. The name was later shortened to Isola Bella. In 1631 Carlo employed the architect Giovanni Angelo Crivelli, and, according to a letter in the family archives, asked him to create 'architecture that is gallant to see and comfortable and gracious to enjoy'.

Neither Carlo nor Giovanni Angelo Crivelli were to live to see the completion of the garden in 1671. It is Carlo's son, Vitaliano VI Borromeo, whose enigmatically smiling portrait hangs in the medal room of the palace, who is considered to be the garden's true founder. Before he took on responsibility for Isola Bella, in around 1650, Vitaliano had had a varied career as an officer, a diplomat and an author of moral and philosophical pamphlets. He developed Crivelli's plans, hiring architect Francesco Castelli as well as many other experts, such as the architect Carlo Fontana and the well-known engineer Mora Toreggio of Rome, who built the water works. The large group of craftsmen that he hired – bricklayers, stone masons, carpenters, painters and architects – were to work on the palace and the garden for another thirty years.

Vitaliano built on the work that had been done under his father. To build the raised areas and terraces, stone from the mountains around the lake had to be transported to the island by ship. Vitaliano also brought over ornaments such as statues, obelisks, balustrades and monumental vases. According to letters in the family archives, Gilbero III, Vitaliano's brother, followed his progress closely, constantly suggesting improvements. He wrote that he wanted the statues to be bigger than a man, so that they could be seen on their pedestals from every corner of the garden. Statues holding sceptres were placed in the corners of all the top terraces, along with plume-crested obelisks.

The grottoes are the biggest surprise – quite unlike anything I've ever seen before. Vitaliano had six of them built in the vaults below the palace, using pebbles in different shades of black and white to form delicate mosaics. They are reminiscent of the nymphaea of Antiquity, the man-made grottoes dedicated to the nymphs (spirits of nature) that were common in the gardens of the Renaissance and the Baroque. On a hot day it is refreshing to walk around in the cool semi-darkness and take a closer look at the decorations and the sea-inspired motifs: shells, corals, sea gods, dolphins and turtles. In one grotto, Venus – the goddess of love and beauty – sleeps on a bed of marble and walnut.

The garden was planned in a Baroque style with geometrical forms, topiary shrubs and plantings inspired by French embroidered parterres, along with artistic fountains and marble statues. But in one respect the layout of Isola Bella differs fundamentally from other formal gardens of the time. The central path of the garden, the main axis, is not straight but has to turn sharply in the middle of the island to accommodate the island's irregular shape. This is obvious on a drawing but not easily seen by the naked eye. The architects have cleverly hidden the exact spot where this occurs, just outside the exit to the garden from the palace. In an atrium, where a statue of Diana stands, twin staircases imperceptibly change the direction of the path, realigning the axis of the garden.

Constructed of grey granite, tufa stone, black flint-like pebbles and lime concrete, the Massimo Theatre, a semicircular water theatre in several tiers, forms the end of the higher terraces. In niches are many marble statues, which you can either imagine as sailors or passengers on the ship that forms the island, or appreciate as symbolic figures from mythology – a fascinating subject for people in the seventeenth century. Under the Massimo Theatre is a large cistern that supplies the plants in the garden with water.

From the top terrace there are splendid views of the whole garden. To the south, in the 'stern' of the ship, is the Garden of Love, beautifully laid out in box in patterns arranged in four quarters. The terraces are linked by trellises covered with climbers and lemons, cedars, roses and oleanders (in winter the lemons and cedars are protected by mobile glasshouses to help them survive the colder weather).

In front of the theatre, peacocks strut proudly up and down the lawn. Their heads are crowned by elegant crests and as they spread their beautiful tail feathers to impress, you can hear their distinctive shrill cries. The rare white peacock was brought from Southeast Asia to Europe in the seventeenth century to enhance the parks of the European aristocracy, and to a large extent it was the Borromeo family who introduced peacocks to the area around Lake Maggiore.

I leave the garden, realizing that nothing in the whole world compares to Isola Bella – unless, perhaps, you liken the island to the pyramids of Egypt.

Opposite Princess Bona Borromeo, a descendant of the founders of the garden, described for me the symbolism of the figures in the Massimo Theatre: 'At the top of the pyramid there is a colossal statue of a unicorn ridden by Honour, the main heraldic emblem of the Borromeo family. The allegorical figures of Art and Nature flank it. In the central niche there is a giant carved out of tufaceous rock, personifying Verbano (Lake Maggiore); he dominates the figures of the River Ticino and the River Toce, comfortably reclining in their niches on the water skins that represent the rivers. At the lower level, Diana is sitting with a nymph at either side. This scenographic display is framed by four obelisks and by sculptures of the four elements.'

THE BOTANICAL GARDEN AT LAKE MAGGIORE

CREATED BY NEIL BOYD MCEACHARN 1931–40

Villa Taranto

Pallanza

One morning sitting at the breakfast table, 46-year-old Captain Neil Boyd McEacharn was reading *The Times* as usual when he came across an advertisement that was to change his life. For sale was La Crocetta estate near Lake Maggiore in Italy; enquiries regarding its purchase were to be directed to the Marquis Sant'Elia. This was the moment that Captain McEacharn, the future creator of Villa Taranto, found his destiny – and the first seed of an Italian botanical garden.

Villa Taranto sits on the north-eastern corner of the Castagnola promontory in Pallanza. The glittering lake is not far away, even though the water can only be glimpsed from certain parts of the garden. When I visit it is late April and the Feast of the Tulip is taking place. This is the time of year when the gardens at Villa Taranto are at their most beautiful. The 80,000 bulbs planted by the gardeners are flowering and the tulips are a riot of colour, while the mimosas are spreading their seductive scent. It strikes me that the genetic signal in tulips of the same variety must be incredibly strong, to make all of them unfold their petals at exactly the same time. A wonderful planting of crimson tulips in front of a fountain catches my admiring attention. In the background is the mausoleum where Captain McEacharn is buried, along with the family of his friend, the lawyer Cappelletto.

In 1940, after ten years of hard work, the first garden was finished. The plan is similar to that of an English landscape garden. The visitor is encouraged to wander along meandering paths flanked by exotic trees, surrounded by hills and valleys. At Villa Taranto tens of thousands of plants, shrubs and trees grow in an area of forty acres, including thousands of species that are not native to Italy and which were imported by

The *Valletta* – a valley with a meadow of wild flowers and a little bridge – must have reminded Captain McEacharn of the Scottish landscape in which he grew up.

Above Crimson tulips are arranged symmetrically in a border in front of an elegant fountain. In the distance, behind the trees, are even more colourful tulip plantings.

Opposite A modern water staircase with terraced basins is surrounded by geometric planting areas, filled with different flowers depending on the season.

Captain McEacharn from all over the world. In a hothouse, the sensitive *Victoria cruziana*, a water lily from South America, rests in the water. During its flowering period in June and July, it reaches a diameter of 2 metres (6½ feet).

The four miles of paths take you past different types of landscape and planting environment. I follow an ascending path and reach a wonderful place, the romantic *Valletta*, which is a valley with a bridge and a meadow full of what look like naturally growing wild flowers. Gazing under the Roman-style bridge and down towards the garden, I can see pink and white azaleas and rhododendrons.

In the middle of the garden is the villa itself. Visible but private, it is used as the headquarters of the Prefecture of the new Province of Verbano-Cusio-Ossola.

I soon reach a modern water staircase. The water rushes down between the ponds, which are surrounded by grasses and thousands of tulips in different shades. The beds are rigidly rectangular in form and the bulbs all seem to have been planted at precisely the same distance from one another. In July the tulips are replaced by annuals – zinnias, asters, carnations and so on. Near by is a kidney-shaped basin filled with a single type of water lily, and a basin containing lotus flowers. There is an intense variety of flowers in this part of the park, with many differently themed plantings. On the surrounding benches, people sit drinking coffee and eating ice-creams. Children are climbing the unusual handkerchief tree (*Davidia involucrata*), which originates in China. It was planted in 1938 and has reached an impressive size as a 65-year-old.

During the Second World War, Captain McEacharn travelled to Australia, but he returned to the garden when peace was established. Concerned that the garden should survive after his death, but without heirs, he had given Villa Taranto to the Italian nation in 1939. The garden was opened to the public in 1952.

Villa Taranto is beautiful all year round, but the garden's highlight is the flowering of tulips and other bulbs in April and May. The Japanese magnolias are also at their most stunning in April. At the end of July, when more than 300 varieties of dahlia with varied and colourful petals burst into flower, there is an annual flower show. The dahlias remain in bloom until October, when Villa Taranto closes for the season.

RENAISSANCE VILLA WITH A WATER STAIRCASE
CREATED FOR THE MOZZONI FAMILY 1550S

Villa Cicogna Mozzoni

Bisúschio

Villa Cicogna Mozzoni is to be found in the village of Bisúschio, south of Lake Lugano and next to the mountains. Like many other fifteenth-century Lombardian villas, it was originally a lodge for the entertainment of guests hunting bear in the local woods. When Angela, the only descendant of the Mozzoni family, married Giovan Pietro Cicogna in the mid-sixteenth century, her father Ascanio commissioned the rebuilding of the country estate in the Renaissance style.

From the inner courtyard, with its richly decorated loggia, you reach a sunken garden. This is made up of two square box parterres and rectangular fishponds with fountains surrounded by balustrades. Up some stairs is the next terrace, where the foot of a steep water staircase can be found. It is still impressive, although no longer filled with water, and provides a focal point for the view from the windows of the villa's salons. These rooms contain *trompe l'oeil* frescoes from the 1560s that are similar to those at Villa Farnesina in Rome, illustrating garlands of flowers, vegetables and topiary features.

At the very top of the hill, where the water staircase ends, is a small pavilion silhouetted against the sky that offers magnificent views across the town and the surrounding landscape. In the distance, the glittering waters of the lake can be glimpsed between the trees.

Left The view from the top of the hill takes in the town of Bisúschio and the surrounding landscape, including a glimpse of Lake Lugano. The sunken Renaissance garden is hidden behind dense hedges and a balustrade.

Above On the hillside above the garden is a sixteenth-century water staircase. An avenue of cypresses draws the eye to the pavilion at the top of the hill. Today the staircase is dry, but in its heyday it was filled with fresh water and was one of the most famous of its kind in Italy.

THE DREAM OF THE CLASSICAL GARDEN

CREATED BY SILVIO DELLA VALLE DI CASANOVA AND SOFIA BROWNE 1896–1916

Above Inside the dream-like orangeries, once used for growing citrus fruit, lush greenery and creeping figs (*Ficus pumila*) can be found.

Opposite The palatial house and the jasmine-covered terraces seen from below. Classical statues, obelisks, tall trees and box cut into many different shapes represent an ideal of the Classical Italian garden.

Villa San Remigio

Pallanza

Villa San Remigio is not as well known or as grand as its neighbour Villa Taranto (see page 188), but it has a very romantic history. The story of the garden began in the 1800s when a carriage carrying the Brownes, a family from Ireland, met with an accident in the Pallanza area. While waiting for repairs to be completed, the family discovered the charming hilltop chapel of San Remigio, with its superb views over Lake Maggiore, and the Browne daughters managed to persuade their father to buy the estate.

While still young, Mr Browne's grand-daughter Sofia, an artist, fell in love with her cousin Silvio Della Valle di Casanova, a poet and composer. They married in 1896. Their dream was to transform her grandfather's country estate into an elegant Classical Italian garden. They terraced the steep hillside and divided the garden into areas with different atmospheres: there were gardens themed around sadness, happiness, memory and scent, as well as a *hortus conclusus*. All their artistic talents were used in the creation of the garden, from the use of colour to the choice of fountains and sculptures.

Silvio and Sofia employed forty gardeners, but today only four people manage the entire garden. Giant rhododendrons and azaleas grow here, as well as exotic trees like the *Cryptomeria japonica* planted a hundred years ago. The terrace walls are covered in fragrant false jasmine. Inside the evocative abandoned orangeries, there are maidenhair trees (*Ginkgo biloba*) and creeping figs (*Ficus pumila*).

Villa San Remigio is the perfect place to end this journey through the history of Italian gardens. It is a romantic interpretation of the Classical Italian garden, containing everything that a northern European might envisage when dreaming of Italy: the villa and garden have views across the lake, forest and mountains, and there are even sculptures to represent the gods and goddesses of Antiquity. In this vision of the garden, the location and the views are as important as the plants themselves.

Visiting the Gardens

It is advisable to telephone the garden or the local tourist information office before your visit, as the opening times given here may change. Many of the gardens are closed on Monday, and some may close – or open for longer hours – on public holidays. Entrance fees are approximately €2–12; some gardens are free of charge. Enjoy your visit, but please respect the gardens. Most of the estates are privately owned, with no financial support from the State or elsewhere.

LAZIO

1. Hadrian's Villa
(Villa Adriana)
Via Villa Adriana 204
00019 Tivoli (Roma)
Tel: 0774 382733/530203
Open all year, except on major public holidays.

2. Villa Lante
Via J. Barozzi 71
01031 Bagnaia (VT)
Tel: 0761 288008
Open all year except on public holidays. Guided tours every half an hour.

3. Giardino di Ninfa
Via Ninfina
04010 Doganella di Ninfa (Latina)
Tel: 0773 633935/354241
E-mail: giardini-ninfa@libero.it/ fondazione.caetani@libero.it
Open April–October, on the first weekend and third Sunday of the month (guided tours only; English-speaking guides must be booked in advance). Group visits may be arranged at other times.

4. Villa d'Este
Piazza Trento 1
00019 Tivoli (Roma)
Tel: 0774 332920
E-mail: info@villadestetivoli.info
Website: www.villadestetivoli.info
Open all year except on major public holidays.

5. Villa Borghese
Piazza Scipione Borghese 5
00197 Roma
Tel: 06 82077304
Website: www.villaborghese.it
The park of Villa Borghese is open every day, giardini segreti *by guided tour selected mornings April–October. Groups must book in advance.*

6. Sacro Bosco at Villa Orsini
01020 Bomarzo (VT)
Tel: 0761 924029
Website: www.bomarzo.net
Open all year.

7. Giardini della Landriana
loc. Tor San Lorenzo
Via Campo di Carne 51
00040 Ardea
Tel: 039 6081551/6 91014140
E-mail: info@landriana.com
Website: www.giardinidellalandriana.it
Open April–October at weekends. Group and school visits during the week, booking required.

8. Villa Farnese
Piazza Farnese
01032 Caprarola (VT)
Tel: 0761 646052
Open every morning. Longer opening hours on public holidays.

9. Castello Ruspoli
Piazza della Repubblica 9
01039 Vignanello (VT)
Tel: 0761 755338
E-mail: castelloruspoli@libero.it

Open April–October on Sundays and public holidays. By appointment only in July and August.

10. San Liberato
loc. San Liberato
Via Settevene Palo 33 (km 20)
00062 Bracciano (Roma)
Tel: 06 9988343/99805460
E-mail: info@sanliberato.it
Website: www.sanliberato.it

Open April–October on the first and last Sunday of the month. Open in November on the first and second Sunday of the month only. Closed August and public holidays. Groups welcome by prior booking.

11. Palazzo Patrizi
Castel Giuliano
00062 Bracciano (Roma)
Tel: 06 9987399/99802530

Open April–November. By appointment only, except during the Feast of Roses (usually third weekend in May).

12. Orto Botanico
Largo Cristina di Svezia 24
Trastevere 00165 (Roma)
Tel: 06 6864193
Open every day except on Sunday and Monday and in August. The greenhouses are open in the morning only.

13. Villa Aldobrandini
Via G. Massaia 18
00044 Frascati (Roma)
Tel: 06 9426887
Open every morning except on Sunday (garden only). Visits are by appointment; authorization can be requested at tourist office EPT, Piazza Marconi 1, Frascati, tel. 06 9420331.

CAMPANIA

1. La Mortella
Via F. Calise 39
80075 Forio
Ischia (NA)
Tel: 081 986220/081 986237
E-mail: mortella@pointel.it
Website: www.ischia.it/mortella
Open April–October on Tuesday, Thursday, Saturday and Sunday. Afternoon concerts take place every Saturday and Sunday in the recital hall. Guided tours by request.

2. Villa Il Tritone
Via Marina Grande 5
80067 Sorrento (NA)
Tel: 06 6865152
ritavessichelli@tiscali.it
Open all year, by appointment only.

3. Palazzo Reale
Viale Dohuet 2/A
81100 Caserta
Tel: 0823 448084/277380
E-mail: reggiacaserta@tin.it/caserta@arethusa.net
Open all year, including on public holidays (closed Mondays).

4. Villa Cimbrone
Via Santa Chiara 26
84010 Ravello (SA)
Tel: 089 857459/089 858072
Website: www.villacimbrone.com
Open all year.

5. Villa Rufolo
Piazza Vescovado
84010 Ravello (SA)
Tel: 089 857657/57669
Open all year.

6. Villa San Michele
Viale Axel Munthe
80071 Anacapri (NA)
Tel: 081 8371401
Website: www.sanmichele.org
Open all year.

7. Negombo
Baia di S. Montano
80076 Lacco Ameno
Ischia (NA)
Tel: 081 986152/986055
E-mail: negombo@negombo.it
Website: www.negombo.it
Open all year for use of the thermal baths.

8. Santa Chiara Cloister Garden
Via Benedetto Croce
80121 Napoli
Tel: 081 5526209
Open all year.

9. The Minerva Garden
(Il Giardino della Minerva)
Vicolo F. Sanseverino 25
84100 Salerno
Tel: 089 2586214
This small garden can be difficult to find. It's off Via Torquato Tasso, four blocks above the Villa Comunale (City Hall). Open all year on Tuesday, Thursday, Saturday and public holidays.

TUSCANY

1. Villa Gamberaia
Via del Rossellino 72
50135 Firenze-Settignano
Tel: 055 697205
E-mail: villagam@tin.it
Website: www.villagamberaia.com
Open all year. Guided tours by appointment.

2. La Foce
Strada della Vittoria 61
53042 Chianciano Terme (Siena)
Tel: 0578 69101
E-mail: info@lafoce.com
Website: www.lafoce.com.
Open on Wednesday afternoons only. Group visits can be arranged on weekdays, and may include lunch or tea in the garden.

3. Villa Castello
loc. Castello
Via di Castello 47
50141 Firenze
Tel: 055 454791 (porter's lodge)
Open all year, including public holidays, except on the second and third Monday of the month. Entrance fee includes Villa Petraia.

4. Villa Cetinale
Sovicille
53018 Siena
Tel: 0577 311147
Open by appointment on weekday mornings.

5. Villa Reale
Via Villa Reale
55014 Marlia (Lucca)
Tel: 0583 30108/30009
(tour bookings only)
E-mail: info@parcovillareale.it
Website: www.parcovillareale.it
Open March–November every day except Monday. All other months, groups by appointment only.

6. Venzano
Mazzola
56048 Volterra (PI)
Tel: 0588 39095
E-mail: venzano@sirt.pisa.it
Website: www.venzanogardens.com
Open 1 March–15 December from Thursday–Sunday.

7. Gardens by Pietro Porcinai
By appointment only. Write to Cassetta Postale 106, Ufficio Postale di Firenze Succursale 36, 50135 Firenze.

8. Villa Petraia
loc. Castello
Via della Petraia 40
50141 Firenze
Tel: 055 452691
Open all year, including public holidays, except on the second and third Monday of the month. Entrance fee includes Villa Castello.

9. Villa I Tatti
Via di Vincigliata 26
50135 Firenze
Tel: 055 603251
E-mail: info@itatti.it
Website: www.itatti.it
Very restricted. By appointment only.

10. The Tarot Garden
(Giardino dei Tarocchi)
58100 Garavicchio Capalbio
Tel: 0564 895122/896635
Website: www.nikidesaintphalle.com
Open every afternoon from 1 May–16 October. Group visits (at least 25 people) may be arranged outside this time.

11. The Boboli Gardens
(Giardino di Boboli)
Piazza Pitti 1
50125 Firenze
Tel: 055 294883/2340444
(for guided visits)
Open all year round, including public holidays, except on the first and last Monday of the month.

12. Parco di Demidoff
loc. Pratolino
Via Fiorentina 6
50030 Vaglia (FI)
Tel: 055 409155/409427
E-mail: r.bartolini@provincia.fi.it
Open April–Sept on Thursday–Saturday and public holidays. In March and October open on public holidays only.

13. Villa Mansi
55018 Segromigno
Monte (LU)
Tel: 0583 920234
E-mail: info@villamansi.it
Website: www.villamansi.it
Open every day except Monday. Groups by appointment.

14. Villa Garzoni
Via Castello 1
51014 Collodi Pescia (PT)
Tel: 0572 429590
Open 15 November–15 March, and at weekends at other times of year.

15. Villa Vicobello
Viale Ranuccio Bianchi Bandinelli 14
Strada di Vicobello
53100 Siena
Tel: 0577 248574
E-mail: margherita@vicobello.it
By appointment only.

16. The Carla Fineschi Rose Garden
(Roseto Botanico 'Carla Fineschi')
Fondazione Roseto Botanico
52022 Cavriglia (AR)
Tel: 055 966638
E-mail: info@rosetofineschi.org
Website: www.rosetofineschi.org
You are recommended to visit in May and June, when the roses are in bloom. No prior appointment required.

17. Villa Vignamaggio
Via Petriolo 5
50022 Greve
Tel: 055 854661
E-mail: info@vignamaggio.com
Website: www.vignamaggio.com
Open all year round to guests staying at Villa Vignamaggio. Other visitors should ask at reception for permission to view the grounds.

18. The Iris Garden
(Giardino dell'Iris)
Piazzale Michelangelo
Firenze
Tel: 055 483112 (Società Italiana dell'Iris)
E-mail: segreteria@irisfirenze.it
Website: www.irisfirenze.it
Open 2–20 May; thereafter by appointment only until 5 June. For further information contact the Società Italiana dell'Iris on the telephone number or e-mail address given above, or write to them at Via Bolognese 17, 50139 Firenze.

VENETO

1. Giardino Giusti
Via Giusti 2
37129 Verona
Tel: 045 8034029
Open all year except Christmas.

2. Orto Botanico
Via Orto Botanico 15
35123 Padua
Tel: 049 656614
E-mail: ortobotanico@uni.pd.it
Open April–October.

3. Parco Sigurtà
Via Cavour 1
36067 Valeggio sul Mincio (Verona)
Tel: 045 6371033
E-mail: info@sigurta.it
Website: www.sigurta.it
Open March–November.

4. Villa Rizzardi
loc. Pojega
Via Verdi 4
37011 Bardolino/Negrar (Verona)
Tel: 045 7210028
E-mail: mail@guerrieri-rizzardi.com
Website: www.guerrieri-rizzardi.it
Open April–October. Group visits (minimum 20 people), with wine and olive tasting, can be arranged.

5. Villa Barbaro
Strada Comunale Bassanese
31010 Maser (Treviso)
Tel: 0423 923004
E-mail: villadimaser@tvol.it
Open at weekends and on public holidays; also open on Tuesday in summer. Group visits can be arranged at other times. Closed 24 December–6 January and at Easter.

6. Palazzo Querini Stampalia
Campo Santa Maria Formosa
(Castello 5252)
30122 Venice
Tel: 041 5203433/2711411
Website: www.querinistampalia.it
E-mail: Fondazione@querinistampalia.it
Open every day except Monday.

LIGURIA

1. Villa Hanbury
Corso Montecarlo 43
18038 loc. La Mortola
Ventimiglia (Imperia)
Tel: 0184 229507
E-mail: hanbury@tiscalinet.it
Website: www.amicihanbury.com
Open every day all year round, except on Wednesday from November–March.

2. Villa Durazzo
Via Pallavicini 11–13
16155 Pegli-Genova
Tel: 010 6982865/6982776 (group bookings)
Open all year, every day except Monday. Groups by appointment.

3. The Abbey of La Cervara
Via Cervara 10
(off Lungomare Rossetti)
16038 Santa Margherita Ligure (GE)
Tel: 800652110 (free of charge)
E-mail: visite@cervara.it
Website: www.cervara.it
Accessible by guided tour March–October on the first and third Sunday of the month. Group visits (minimum 30 people) can be arranged during the week.

LOMBARDY AND PIEDMONT

1. Villa Balbianello
Via Comoedia
22016 Lenno
Tel: 0344 56110
Garden open April–October every day except Monday and Wednesday (open on these days too if a public holiday). Access on foot or by boat (on certain days).

2. Villa Carlotta
Via Regina 2
22019 Tremezzo (CO)
Tel: 0344 40405
E-mail: entevillacarlotta@tin.it
Website: www.villacarlotta.it
Open every day April–September. Guided tours must be booked in advance. The garden may be reached on foot and by boat (Cadenabbia landing).

3. Villa Melzi
22021 Bellagio
Loppia (CO)
Tel: 031 951281
Open every day from 27 March–31 October (garden only). The site may be entered from both Bellagio and Loppia.

4. Isola Madre
28050 Isola Madre (VB)
Tel: 0323 31261
Open March–October.
The garden is reached by boat.

5. Isola Bella
28050 Isola Bella (VB)
Tel: 0323 30556
Open March–October. The garden is reached by boat.

6. Villa Taranto
Via V. Veneto 111 Taranto
28922 Verbania Pallanza (VB)
Tel: 0323 404555
E-mail: entevillataranto@tin.it
Website: www.villataranto.it
Open April–October.

7. Villa Cicogna Mozzoni
Piazza Cicogna 8
21050 Bisúschio (VA)
Tel: 0332 471134
E-Mail: eleopaa@tin.it
Website: www.villacicognamozzoni.it
Open April–October and on Sunday and public holidays during the rest of the year. Guided tours every day by appointment.

8. Villa San Remigio
Via S. Remigio 19
28922 Verbania Pallanza (VB)
Tel: 0323 503249/556669
By appointment only.

2115 Spluga
Ortles
3905
Bormio
4049
Verbano-Cusio-Domodossola
Sondrio
3539
L. Maggiore
Adamello
Monte Rosa
-Ossola
4637
Verbania
L. di Como
1 2 3
4+5 6+8
7
Lecco
Varese
Como
Bergamo
Lombardia
L. di Garda
Biella
Ivrea
Novara
Milano
Brescia
Ticino
Vercelli
Oglio
Lodi
Susa
Casale Monferrato
Adda
Pavia
Cremona
Torino
Mantova
Po
Piemonte
Voghera
Po
Asti
Pinerolo
Alessandria
M. Viso
3841
Saluzzo
Alba
Mondovì
Cuneo
1908
Tenda

Bibliography

Here is a selection of works on, or relating to, Italian gardens, which readers wishing to find out more about the subject may find useful. Please note that not all are still in print.

Agnelli, Marella, *Gardens of the Italian Villas*, Weidenfeld and Nicolson (London, 1987)

Barisi, Isabella, Fagiolo, Marcello and Madonna, Luisa, *Villa d'Este*, De Luca Editori d'Arte (Rome, 2003)

Brown, Jane, *The Modern Garden*, Princeton Architectural Press (New York, 2000)

Campitelli, Alberta, *Villa Borghese*, Istituto Poligrafico Zecca dello Stato (Rome, 2003)

Caneva, Giulia and Bohuny, Lorenza, 'Botanical Analysis of the Villa of Livia's Painted Flora', *Journal of Cultural Heritage* 4, II, April 2003

Ciarallo, Annamaria, *Gardens of Pompeii*, J. Paul Getty Trust Publications (Los Angeles, 2002)

Coffin, David R., *The Villa d'Este at Tivoli*, Princeton University Press (Princeton, 1960)

Colonna, Francesco, *Hypnerotomachia Poliphili*: *The Strife of Love in a Dream*, first published 1499; reprinted by Thames and Hudson (London, 2003)

De Saint Phalle, Niki, *The Tarot Garden*, Acatos (Lausanne, 1999)

Du Prey, Pierre de la Ruffinière, *The Villas of Pliny from Antiquity to Posterity*, University of Chicago Press (Chicago and London, 1994)

Fantoni, Marcello, Flores, Heidi and Pfordresher, John (eds), *Cecil Pinsent and his Gardens in Tuscany,* Edifir Edizioni Firenze (Florence, 1996)

Harris, Cyril M. (ed.), *Illustrated Dictionary of Historic Architecture*, Dover Publications (New York, 1977)

Klynne, Allan and Liljenstolpe, Peter, 'Prima Porta: Investigating the Gardens of the Villa of Livia', *Journal of Roman Archaeology* 13, 2000

Lazzaro, Claudia, *The Italian Renaissance Garden*, Yale University Press (New Haven and London, 1990)

Masson, Georgina, *Italian Gardens*, Thames and Hudson (London, 1961)

Matteini, Milena, *Pietro Porcinai: Architetto del Giardino e del Paesaggio*, Electa (Milan, 2004)

Origo, Iris, *Images and Shadows: Part of a Life*, Harcourt Brace Jovanovich (New York, 1970)

Osmond, Patricia J. (ed.), *Revisiting the Gamberaia: An Anthology of Essays*, Centro Di (Florence, 2004)

Page, Russell, *The Education of a Gardener*, Harvill Press (London, 1995)

Palladio, Andrea, *The Four Books of Architecture*, first published 1570; reprinted by Dover Publications (New York, 1976)

Shepherd, J.C. and Jellicoe, G.A., *Italian Gardens of the Renaissance*, first published 1925; reprinted by Princeton Architectural Press (Princeton, 1993)

Van Zuylen, *The Gardens of Russell Page*, Stewart, Tabori & Chang (New York, 1991)

Wharton, Edith, *Italian Villas and their Gardens*, first published 1904; reprinted by Da Capo Press (New York, 1988)

Index

Page numbers in *italic* refer to captions to illustrations

S

T

U

V

W

Y

Z

Acknowledgments

AUTHOR'S ACKNOWLEDGMENTS

Architect MSA (SAR) Bengt Rönnhedh deserves a special mention. He has played an important part in awakening my interest in the architecture of gardens. (During our joint research in Rome, Bengt studied architectural history and building conservation applied to the concept of the Italian villa, as a fellow of the Swedish Institute in Rome from 1999 to 2000). Bengt has been an adviser for this project and I am most grateful for his support.

I would also like to thank Tina Engström, who with great professionalism has translated the book from Swedish to English. She is also a qualified Blue Badge Guide for gardens in the UK and has generously contributed her knowledge to the project.

Thanks also to:

Photographer Åke E:son Lindman

Landscape architect Thorbjörn Andersson

Swedish Institute in Rome (Istituto Svedese di Studi Classici a Roma): Professor Anne-Marie Leander Touati (former Director), Stefania Renzetti, Margareta Ohlson Lepscky, Professor Barbro Santillo Frizell (Director), Associate Professor Börje Magnusson, Allan Klynne, Pia Letalick, Astrid Capoferro and the rest of the staff

The library of the American Academy in Rome

My family – Maj, Lars, Pelle and Lil Larås – and encouraging friends

Anna Andersson and the Italian Government Tourist Board in Stockholm

Madeleine Wulfsson, Brita Carlens, Carla Magnusson, Cecilia Klynne

Landscape architect AgrD Kjell Lundquist, Professor Giorgio Galletti (expert in Medici villas), Professor Elsa M Cappelletti (Orto Botanico), Lena Landgren (expert in Roman botanics)

The publisher Frances Lincoln Ltd in London – in particular Anne Fraser, Becky Clarke and editors Jo Christian and Fiona Robertson. Thank you for your professionalism and your patience.

Finally, my gratitude to the owners of the gardens in Italy, who open their private property to the general public. Thank you for all your hard work managing and caring for an important European cultural heritage.

PHOTOGRAPHIC ACKNOWLEDGMENTS

a = above, b = below, c = centre, l = left, r = right

AKG-Images/Erich Lessing: 12–13

Ann Larås: 4l, 4r, 5c, 5r, 9, 10, 14, 17, 18–19, 26, 27, 29, 30, 32, 33, 34–5, 36, 38, 39, 40, 41, 43, 44, 45, 46, 47, 50, 52, 53, 61, 62, 65, 66, 67, 69, 91ar, 92, 94, 95, 98, 99, 100–101, 108, 109, 110, 111, 112, 114, 115, 118, 119, 120, 121, 122, 123, 124, 125, 126, 127, 128, 129, 130, 131, 132, 133, 135, 136, 137, 138, 139, 145a, 145b, 147, 149, 150, 151, 153, 156–7, 158, 159, 161, 162, 163, 164–5, 166, 169, 171, 172, 175, 176, 177, 179, 180, 181, 182, 183, 184, 185, 186, 188–9, 190, 191, 192, 193, 194, 195

Åke E:son Lindman: 1, 2, 4c, 5l, 20, 22r, 23, 24, 48–9, 54, 55, 56, 57, 58, 59, 70–1, 72–3, 74, 75, 77, 78, 80, 81, 82, 83, 84–5, 86, 87, 88, 89, 91al, 91bl, 91br, 93, 102–103, 105, 107, 116, 117, 140–1, 142, 145c, 154, 155

Negombo Archives: 96

Private Collection: 15, 22l, 37, 42, 96, 104, 144, 146

© 2005 Touring Editore, Milano: 6, 7, 196, 197, 198, 199, 200, 201